Great Adventures for Kitsap Peninsula

Family Fun in the West Sound

By
Christina Rude & Debbie Rue

Illustrated by
Gale Engelke

*Happy Adventuring!
Compliments of
Automotive Alternatives!
Christina*

R & R Publications

Printed by Gorham Printing
Rochester, Washington

ISBN 0-9657914-0-8

Illustrated by Gale Engelke
Special contributions from Beth Cockrel, Dale King, Steve and Cindy Robinson, The Duke's and Allison Rose Engelke

Published by R & R Publications
P. O. Box 133
Silverdale, WA 98383

Printed in Washington State

This book is dedicated to families who invest time with their children and have adventures together. May God bless your family with wonderful memories.

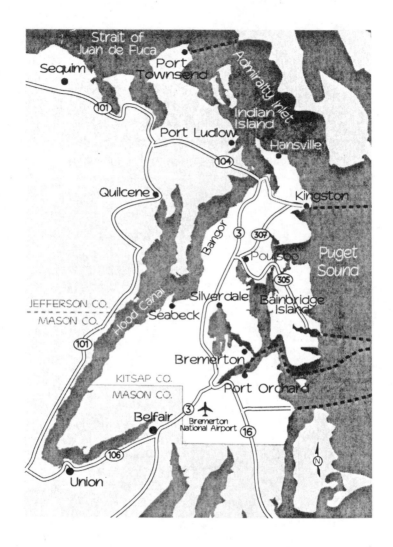

The Kitsap Peninsula has been Puget Sound's best kept secret. For years it has been the gateway to the Olympics or a way to get to Seattle. It quietly lies, unassuming, in the middle of the Puget Sound connecting the Olympic Peninsula with the metropolitan cities of Seattle and Tacoma. With over 236 miles of saltwater shoreline it has a delightful mix of rural and urban towns. This family friendly peninsula will amaze you with its hidden treasures.

TABLE OF CONTENTS

WONDERFUL PARKS

A-HIKING WE WILL GO

With all our beautiful mountains, it's fun to take a hiking adventure with your family, too. This 3-mile hike is fun for everyone. Formed thousands of years ago by a huge rockslide, LOWER LENA LAKE has beautiful scenery you can enjoy today. The trail starts in 50-year-old trees and after a quarter mile enters an old growth forest- really BIG trees. The trail crosses the dry stream bed of Lena Creek at one and a half miles. The elevation is 1800 feet when you reach the shore of Lower Lena Lake. Daring ones may enjoy an invigorating swim in the cold waters.
BRRR...

BEFORE YOU GO
● Wear layered clothes and comfortable
sturdy shoes with heavy socks.
● Bring necessary hiking supplies (extra food,
extra clothing, first aid kit, a pocketknife, matches,
a flashlight, a whistle and a compass).

ON THE WAY
● Talk about hiking in the woods. (Always stay on the
trail, stay with your hiking group, rest frequently,
drink water and eat healthy snacks along the way,
don't eat berries or mushrooms, don't drink the creek
water, pack your litter out and practice common sense.)

HELPFUL INFORMATION
● Take Highway 3 to Gorst, staying in the right lane. At
Gorst follow signs to Bremerton Nt'l Airport (Hwy 3S)
and Belfair. Go through Belfair and connect to Highway
101S. Go a mile north of the Hamma Hamma River bridge.
Go uphill on Hamma Hamma River Road #25. At 9.5 miles
from the highway you'll arrive at the Lena Lake trailhead,
elevation 685 feet.
● Have your children take turns being the leader, it will
increase the energy of your hikers.
● Relax, take your time and have patience. A hike is
sweeter when filled with encouraging words and praise.
Remember the fun is THE HIKE.

MAKING MEMORIES
Help your children make a picture with chocolate
instant pudding. What you'll need:
   chocolate instant pudding
   white paper
   newspaper
   clean hands
Prepare the pudding according to the package
directions. Place a piece of paper over newspaper. Finger-paint or make
handprints and even footprints. Your children can lick their fingers clean!

3

SITTIN' ON THE DOCK OF THE BAY

In the heart of old Silverdale, there lies a great place for outdoor exploring. The SILVERDALE WATERFRONT PARK is the place where you can play on a great playground, roller-skate, pitch horseshoes and see the Farmer's Market on weekends. Find the crabs on the sidewalk and have your children make a rubbing to take home. Count how many steps it takes to get to the end of the dock. If you step out onto the floating piers you can peer into the water and spy an interesting underwater community.

BEFORE YOU GO

- Wear layered clothes and old tennis shoes for walking on the rocky beach.
- Bring paper and pencil for a sidewalk rubbings.
- Bring roller-skates and rollerblades. Don't forget your helmet.

ON THE WAY

- Did you know Silverdale Bay is part of the Puget Sound? In the fall, many salmon come back to spawn in the nearby creeks that run into the Puget Sound.

HELPFUL INFORMATION

- Silverdale Waterfront Park is located in Old Silverdale.
- Take Highway 3 to the Newberry Hill exit. Go East into Silverdale. Turn right at Byron Street. Silverdale Waterfront Park is at the end of Byron Street on the right.
- Silverdale Waterfront Park is open year round, dawn to dusk.

MAKING MEMORIES

Make a fish bowl feast for dessert tonight. What you'll need:
  a new or clean unused fish bowl
  blue raspberry or lime Jell-O
  gummy fish or Gumi worms
Mix the blue raspberry or lime Jell-O in a very clean fish bowl. After the Jell-O cools add gummy fish or worms. Once the gelatin sets, the bowl will look like an underwater community. For extra fun, add cool whip for white caps.

KIDS AND KITES

Take a drive up to Port Townsend for a
high-flying adventure. FORT WORDEN STATE
PARK offers the perfect location for kite flying
with beautiful surroundings. You'll find a long
stretch of beach with just enough wind. Play on
the driftwood, picnic in the sand and explore
old army bunkers. Be sure to drive over to the
military cemetery, a great place to get rubbings.
If you're not too tired, enjoy the quaint shops
along the waterfront of Port Townsend.
There's delicious homemade ice cream at
the ELEVATED ICE CREAM SHOP.

BEFORE YOU GO

- Bring a lunch or snacks and water.
- Bring a jacket, extra clothing and kites (or buy them in Pt. Townsend).
- Bring flashlights for exploring the army bunkers.
- Bring paper and crayons for rubbing.

ON THE WAY

- As you travel across the Hood Canal Bridge, watch for any submarines traveling to Bangor.
- Did you know that Fort Worden was the location for the film "An Officer and a Gentleman"?

HELPFUL INFORMATION

- Take Highway 3N to Highway 104W across the Hood Canal Bridge. Continue on to Highway 101N and then to Highway 20 to Port Townsend. Turn left onto Kearney Street. Follow signs to Fort Worden State Park.
- Fort Worden State Park is open year round, dawn to dusk. 1-800-233-0321
- The place to get a rubbing is the military cemetery. Follow signs in Fort Worden, going to the end of the road, past the tent camping sites.
- In Port Townsend, the Elevated Ice Cream Shop is at 627 Water Street and is open daily 9 am - 10 pm. (360) 385-1156

MAKING MEMORIES

Help your children make a kite poem; it's as easy as 1,2,3,4,5.

Line 1 has one word that gives the title.	Kite
Line 2 has two words that tell about the title.	Windy, Funny
Line 3 has three words that make a phrase.	In the Sky
Line 4 has four words that tell about the title.	Twirling, Flying, Soaring, Diving
Line 5 has one word that summarizes the idea.	Fun

For extra fun, write your kite poem on kite-shaped paper.
Did you know you just wrote a French poem called a Cinquain?

THE SECRET GARDEN

It's the ANNA SMITH CHILDREN'S PARK in Silverdale. Master Gardeners cultivate a beautiful demonstration garden there. Your children can play in the bean pole tepee, tell time with the sundial and see the worm bin. What is written on the arbor at the entrance to the garden? Find the nearby path and venture down to the water. On the way, stop at the amphitheater and use your imagination for singing, dancing or maybe a silly fashion show. At the water's edge, skip rocks, walk along the shoreline or dip your toes in Silverdale Bay.

BEFORE YOU GO
●Bring a lunch or snacks and water.
●Bring a jacket.

ON THE WAY
●Count all the different kinds of flowers you see in bloom.

HELPFUL INFORMATION
●Anna Smith Children's Park is located near the intersection of Tracyton Boulevard and Fairgrounds Road in Silverdale.
●Take Highway 3 to Highway 303S exit/Waaga Way.
Take Waaga Way to Ridgetop Boulevard exit. Go west on Ridgetop Boulevard and left at the first light, Myhre. Continue on Myhre, it turns into Tracyton Boulevard.
●Parking is across the street on Fairgrounds Road.
●The Anna Smith Children's Park is open year round, dawn to dusk.
●Master Gardeners are available on Wednesdays for tours or any gardening questions-just ask.

MAKING MEMORIES
Help your children build their own crystal garden. What you'll need:
    small pieces (walnut size) of brick
    small pieces of briquettes (coal)
    6 TBS. bluing (find it near the
    laundry soaps at the store)
    6 TBS. non-iodized salt
    6 TBS. water, 3 TBS. ammonia
    Fairly deep bowl or jar, food coloring,
    tiny twigs or toothpicks, plastic flowers, tiny houses

Wet the bricks and briquette pieces and place them in the bowl. Prop the twigs between the brick and briquette pieces. Arrange plastic flowers on the briquettes. Mix the bluing, 3 TBS. salt, ammonia and water in a cup. Slowly pour the mixture over the brick and briquette pieces in the bowl. Drop a few drops of food coloring on the tops of your "garden." Sprinkle the remaining 3 TBS. of salt evenly over the garden. Add flowers and houses. Place your town in a warm place where it will not be disturbed. In a few hours, a "coral-like" growth of crystals will begin to form on the bricks, making an interesting garden. To keep your garden growing, add one TBS. ammonia to it once a week.

THERE'S GOLD IN THEM THAR HILLS

This is a great hike for kids of all ages. The GOLD CREEK trail to the Green Mountain Vista is a hike about two and a half miles long, with a climb over 1000 feet. The trailhead begins near Lake Symington at the southern end of Lake Tahuya. It starts with a fairly easy ascent and has short spurts of a moderate grade-nothing the kids will complain about for very long. The hike begins beside Gold Creek, then rises above it, continuing up to the summit. This vista at 1690 feet has incredible views of Seattle, Mt. Rainier, Bremerton and the Olympics. For extra fun, hunt for gold in the creek.

BEFORE YOU GO

- Wear layered clothes and comfortable sturdy shoes with heavy socks.
- Bring a lunch or snacks and water (there are picnic tables available below the summit).
- Bring necessary hiking supplies (extra food, extra clothing, first aid kit, a pocketknife, matches, a flashlight, a whistle and a compass).

ON THE WAY

- Talk about hiking in the woods. (Always stay on the trail, stay with your hiking group, rest frequently, drink water and eat healthy snacks along the way, don't eat berries or mushrooms, don't drink the creek water, pack your litter out and practice common sense.)

HELPFUL INFORMATION

- Take Highway 3 to the Newberry Hill exit. Turn west and follow Newberry Hill to the end of the road. Turn left onto Seabeck Highway. Take a right on Holly Road.
- There is parking off the road on the left side, along with a fixed map at the trailhead.
- Green Mountain trails are open year round, dawn to dusk. 1-800-527-3305
- Have your children take turns being the leader, it will increase the energy of your hikers.
- Relax, take your time and have patience. A hike is sweeter when filled with encouraging words and praise. Remember the fun is THE HIKE.

MAKING MEMORIES

Make some gold nuggets together. What you'll need:

1 pkg. butterscotch chips, $\frac{3}{4}$ cup creamy peanut butter
3$\frac{1}{2}$ cups (7oz) mini marshmallows, 1 can (8.5 oz) chow mein noodles
Melt the butterscotch chips in the microwave for 1 minute, stir. Melt them at 10 second intervals, stirring until smooth, then add peanut butter. Stir in the marshmallows and noodles, until evenly coated. Drop by spoonfuls on waxed paper and chill until your gold diggers are hungry.

MILLION DOLLAR VIEW

You're in for a grand surprise if you've never been to SCENIC BEACH STATE PARK. This country get-away will treat you to breathtaking vistas of the Olympic Mountains rising out of the water in front of you. Explore the oyster-filled beach, picnic in areas with sun or shade, and play at the large playground. Find the old log cabin by the playground and read the plaque to discover who lived there first. Explore the trails through the woods. Along the beach your children can actually stand under tree roots. Enjoy this million dollar view; it's quite a treasure.

BEFORE YOU GO
- Wear layered clothes and old tennis shoes for walking on the rocky beach.
- Bring a lunch or snacks and water.
- Bring Band-aids for oyster scrapes.

ON THE WAY
- Can you see the Olympic Mountains?
- Find Mt. Constance and The Brothers. (Where do you suppose The Sisters are?)

HELPFUL INFORMATION
- Scenic Beach State Park is in Seabeck.
- Take Highway 3 to the Newberry Hill exit. Turn west and follow Newberry Hill to the end of the road. Turn right onto Seabeck Highway. Travel through Seabeck, and a half a mile from the post office, take a right on Scenic Beach Road. The park is located 1.3 miles down on the right. This park is very well marked with signs.
- Scenic Beach State Park is open March 13 - September 30, dawn to dusk. 1-800-223-0321

MAKING MEMORIES
Watch a sunset over the Olympic Mountains together.

LIGHTHOUSE ACTION

You'll find action up north exploring a great sandy beach, chasing waves back & forth, flying kites in the wind and watching boats at POINT NO POINT. See Kitsap County's only lighthouse, Point No Point Lighthouse, built in 1878, which is a National Historic Site. Your children can even fish off the beach if they want. After your beach exploration, enjoy a cool treat at KOUNTRY KORNER, where you'll find giant chainsaw carvings. Take your children's picture next to their favorite carving. Do they like the fishman, the eagle or the bear with a hamburger?

BEFORE YOU GO
- Wear layered clothes and bring extra socks, shoes or pants for children who play too close to the water.
- Bring a lunch or snacks and water.
- Bring your camera and fishing gear.

ON THE WAY
- Enjoy the country drive. Watch for scenic valleys with silos and cows.
- Talk about why lighthouses are needed.
- On Point No Point Road, can you find the house that is the top of a ferry?
- Watch for eagles.

HELPFUL INFORMATION
- Take Highway 3 to 305S (Poulsbo exit). Continue on Highway 305S and go left at Bond Road (307N). Follow Bond Road to Hansville Highway, turning left. Travel 5 miles to Point No Point County Road. Turn right to the dead end. Hopefully parking will be available.
- Tours of the lighthouse are available every weekend, May - September, 12 pm - 4 pm.
- When you're done at the beach, retrace your path to Kountry Korner which is on the corner of Hansville Highway and Bond Road.

MAKING MEMORIES

Your children can make binoculars to watch for ships. What you'll need:
    two empty toilet paper rolls
    tape, yarn or string
    crayons or contact paper
Decorate the toilet paper rolls with crayons or contact paper. Tape the two rolls together. Use string or yarn to attach a shoulder strap. Your children can use the binoculars at the beach to "sea" new things.

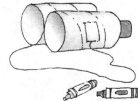

FIND BURIED TREASURES

The rocky beach and tide pools at KITSAP MEMORIAL PARK are full of hidden treasures. Tiny crabs, starfish, limpets, chitons, and other marine life are just waiting to be discovered by your young adventurers. Do you know what animal is protected by the white plastic tubes on the beach? Enjoy a large grassy field (baseball or soccer, anyone?), a playground, volleyball courts and horseshoe pits. Outdoor grills and shaded picnic areas can provide a place for a great barbecue.

BEFORE YOU GO

- Wear layered clothes and old tennis shoes for walking on the rocky beach.
- Bring a lunch or snacks and water.
- Bring horseshoes, Frisbees, baseball, volleyball or soccer equipment.

ON THE WAY

- Talk about what marine life you might see.
  Repeat the "Beach Pledge" by the Marine Science Society of the Pacific Northwest:
  "When I go to the beach, I will remember that I am a guest. If I turn over rocks to look at what lives beneath them, I will carefully put the rock back just how I found it. I know that rocks provide homes to many animals and plants. I will take home memories, photos, and sketches and leave only footprints in the sand. I will take actions in my daily life to reduce pollutants entering Puget Sound, thereby protecting Puget Sound and its rich community of plants and animals."

HELPFUL INFORMATION

- Take Highway 3 toward the Hood Canal. Kitsap Memorial State Park is on the left, well marked with signs. (360) 779-3205
- Kitsap Memorial State Park is open year round, 8 am to dusk.

MAKING MEMORIES

Help your children start a rock collection at home. Look for really special rocks, very dark or light in color, smooth, heart shaped, or round. Think of fun ways to display the collection.

DISCOVERING THE JEWEL OF GUILLEMOT

Very few people have heard of
GUILLEMOT COVE NATURE RESERVE.
Described by the Parks Department as a
164-acre jewel on the Hood Canal, this adventure
is a wonderful outing and an enjoyable family hike.
This one-mile trail goes down through the woods
to a field with a barn. Across the field is a bridge
which will take you to another meadow. Can you
find the stumphouse hidden in the woods?
(Legend says an escaped convict used this
treehouse as a hideout for a couple of years!)
Continue on to a cabin and to a beautiful beach
with a stunning view of the Olympics. Take a
short break on the way back up the trail and make
rubbings using the big beautiful maple leaves along
the path. Did you know these maple leaves are
some of the biggest on the Olympic peninsula?

BEFORE YOU GO

- Wear layered clothes and old tennis shoes for walking along the beach.
- Bring a lunch or snacks and water.
- Restroom facilities are limited, so plan ahead.
- Bring band-aids for oyster scrapes.
- Bring crayons and paper for a maple leaf rubbing.

ON THE WAY

- Enjoy the country drive up and down hills, through the different trees. Can you tell the difference between an evergreen and a deciduous tree?

HELPFUL INFORMATION

- Take Highway 3 to the Newberry Hill exit. Turn west and follow Newberry Hill to the end of the road. Turn right onto Seabeck Highway. Travel through Seabeck and a half mile past the Post Office; take a right on Scenic Beach Road. After .5 miles, turn left on Stavis Bay Road. The park is 4.4 miles on the left. Parking is on the right.
- No pets or bikes.
- Reservations are NOT required (contrary to posted signs), unless there are more than 25 people in your group.
- Guillemot Cove Nature Reserve is open September - April, weekends, 9 am - 5 pm; May - August, daily, 9 am - 5 pm.
- Admission is FREE.
- For more information or reservations call (360) 895-3895 (weekdays) or (360) 830-0159 (weekends).

MAKING MEMORIES

Make a leaf rubbing together. What you'll need:
  white unlined paper
  dark green or black crayons
  maple leaves

Place the leaf, bottom up, on a smooth hard surface. Put paper over the leaf and hold firmly. Make strokes with the side of the crayon, back and forth, from top to bottom so veins and margins of the leaf appear.

KITSAP'S UNKNOWN SOLDIER

Families don't have to travel far to see the Tomb
of the Unknown Soldier. Tucked away in the
IVY GREEN CEMETERY in West Bremerton is
a big white monument honoring the unidentified
soldiers who gave their lives for our country.
As you explore the cemetery, you will have to
hunt for this monument because it is not easily
found. This cemetery is rich in local history, so
imagine the life of a pioneer as you wander
through the tombstones. As you find interesting
gravemarkers, make rubbings for a keepsake.
Find a veteran's grave and leave a flag or
flower on it to honor their sacrifice. Afterwards
enjoy a delicious milkshake at NOAH'S ARK
RESTAURANT.

BEFORE YOU GO
●Bring a flag or flowers.
●Bring crayons and paper for grave rubbings.

ON THE WAY
●Talk about freedom. What is it? Why have Americans been willing to die to preserve it?

HELPFUL INFORMATION
●Ivy Green Cemetery is locaated at 1401 Naval Avenue in Bremerton.
●Take Highway 3 to the Kitsap Way exit. Turn east on Kitsap Way. Travel 2 miles, turning left on 11th Street. Turn left again at Naval Avenue. The Ivy Green Cemetery is on the left, one block down.
●The tomb of the unknown soldier is on the SE corner of the cemetery, up on the hill.
●The Ivy Green Cemetery Park is open year round, dawn to dusk. (360) 478-5355
●Noah's Ark Restaurant is at 1516 6th Street. (360) 377-8110

MAKING MEMORIES
Help your children make a rubbing of a gravemarker that they like. They can use their imagination and write or tell a story about a family or soldier buried at Ivy Green Cemetery.

COMBING THE BEACHES AT MANCHESTER

Do you have any beachcombers in your family? Take them to MANCHESTER STATE PARK in Port Orchard and let them discover seaside treasures in hidden coves. This beach site also has a huge sheltered picnic area which, built in 1904, once stored torpedoes. Your children will be delighted to find and explore an old mining casemate on the beach. This building was used to test mines in Rich Passage. When you're finished exploring, play games together on the grassy fields or walk on the 1½ miles of trails.

BEFORE YOU GO
•Wear old tennis shoes for walking on the rocky beach.
•Bring flashlights for exploring the casemate building.

ON THE WAY
•As you drive along the Port Orchard waterfront, watch
for a gigantic wood carving of a fisherman
(3600 Beach Drive).

HELPFUL INFORMATION
•Manchester State Park is located in Port Orchard.
•Take Highway 3 to Highway 16E (Port Orchard). Stay
in your left lane and go through the downtown area.
Turn left on Bay Drive and travel 5.2 miles. (Bay
Drive turns into Beach Drive.) Manchester State Park
is on the left. 1-800-233-0321
•Manchester State Park is open April 1 - September 30,
dawn to dusk.

MAKING MEMORIES
Make Beach Blobs for your explorers. What you'll need:
    1 cup brown rocks (or you may use chocolate chips)
    2 cups oyster shells (or you may use oatmeal)
    $\frac{1}{2}$ cup seaweed (or you may use green tinted coconut)
    $\frac{1}{4}$ cup chopped driftwood (or you may use nuts)
    $\frac{1}{2}$ cup goo (or you may use butter)
    2 cups white sand (or you may use sugar)
    $\frac{1}{2}$ cup beach water (or you may use milk)
    1 tsp. diluted mud (or you may use vanilla)
Mix first four ingredients in a
large bowl. Mix the goo, sand
and beach water together in a
saucepan. Bring to a rolling boil
over low heat. Remove from
heat and add diluted mud. Pour
this liquid over the rock mixture.
Drop from teaspoon onto wax
paper. Your beachcombers
will really enjoy this creation!

PICK A LAKE, ANY LAKE!

What summer would be complete without a trip to the lake? There are MANY lakes to choose from in Kitsap County, each with its own personality. BUCK LAKE has a large swimming area, huge fields for running, playgrounds, fishing, and a boat launch. ISLAND LAKE has a perfect area for younger kids, with a roped-off swimming section and a big sandy beach. Bring bikes along or walk the path through nature trails. WILDCAT LAKE has a great playtoy for older kids, a roped-off swimming area with a sloped grassy spot and picnic places above the beach. KITSAP LAKE is a great place for boating and fishing. A smaller swimming area and picnic facilities are found there. LONG LAKE has a BIG grassy field to play on, a large playtoy and big sandy beaches with shallow waters for swimming. This is also a good lake for boating and fishing. There are no lifeguards on duty at any of these lakes. Enjoy exploring all these lakes and see which one is the best for your family.

BEFORE YOU GO

- Pack for your family; include extra clothing, beach chairs, towels, beach toys, camera, bubble soap, fishing gear, inner tubes or boats.
- If you plan on swimming, call the Health Department to see if the lake you want to go to has "swimmer's itch." (360) 478-5285

ON THE WAY

- As you drive to the "L"ake, count how many things you see that begin with "L."

HELPFUL INFORMATION

- Some lakes that are worth checking out include:
  - BUCK LAKE: Take Highway 3 to 305S (Poulsbo exit). Continue on Highway 305S and go left at Bond Road (307N). Follow Bond Road to Hansville Highway, turning left. Travel 5 miles and left. Buck Lake is on the left. FREE
  - ISLAND LAKE: Take Highway 3 to Highway 303S to Waaga Way. Take the Ridgetop Boulevard exit. Turn east, traveling on Ridgetop Boulevard for 2 miles. Turn right on Gallery and then right onto Island Lake Road which curves around to the park. FREE
  - WILDCAT LAKE: Take Highway 3 to the Newberry Hill exit. Turn west and follow Newberry Hill to the end of the road. Turn left onto Seabeck Highway. Turn right onto Holly Road, traveling about a mile to Wildcat Lake on left. FREE
  - KITSAP LAKE: Take Highway 3 to the Chico Way exit. Go south on Chico Way until it turns into Kitsap Way. Turn right on Harlow and right on Price to Kitsap Lake Park. FREE
  - LONG LAKE: Take Highway 3 to Gorst. Follow the signs to Highway 16E (Tacoma) and take the Sedgwick exit. Go left off the freeway onto Sedgwick to Long Lake Road and watch for signs. FREE

MAKING MEMORIES

Have some bubble fun with bubble soap using different wands. Bend a wire hanger into a circle or different loop shapes. Try using a fish net, a fly swatter or a strawberry basket from the store. Pour the bubble liquid on a pie pan and using different wands see the big bubbles appear.

STROLL ON THE SPIT

Take a stroll with birds and other wildlife along the DUNGENESS SPIT NATURE RESERVE. Over six miles of beautiful sandy beach is shared with hundreds of bird species. You'll see the great blue herons, mallards and maybe an eagle overhead. Your adventure begins with a trail in the forest and comes down out onto the sandy beach full of driftwood. Your kids can "use" a walking stick while they are there, but there is no driftwood collecting at this reserve. Look for different tracks in the sand. Remember the weather in Sequim is usually much nicer, so any day can have the potential to be a great one at this spit.

BEFORE YOU GO

- Wear layered clothes, bring a hat or sunglasses and extra socks, shoes or pants for children who play too close to the water.
- Bring a picnic lunch or snacks and water.
- Bring your binoculars, bird books, pencils and paper.

ON THE WAY

- As you begin your drive have your children list all the birds, animals, buildings, or things they MIGHT see on this adventure. Your children can cross off the items if they are seen on the way.

HELPFUL INFORMATION

- Take Highway 3N to Highway 104W across the Hood Canal Bridge. Continue on Highway 104W to Highway 101N and travel through Sequim. About 4.5 miles west of Sequim turn right on Kitchen-Dick Lane. Follow the signs 3 miles to the Dungeness Recreation Area and Dungeness National Wildlife Refuge.
- The Dungeness National Wildlife Refuge is open year round, dawn to dusk. (360) 457-8451
- No Frisbees, kites or pets.
- Admission: $2.00 per family.

MAKING MEMORIES

Help your children make edible "snacklaces" for themselves and the birds at home. String some cereal with yarn and tie the ends to make a necklace or bracelet or hang it out in a tree.

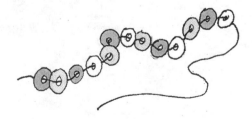

BATTLE FOR POINTS
AT THE
BATTLEPOINT PARK

Tennis, anyone? There are wonderful tennis courts waiting for up and coming tennis pros at BATTLEPOINT PARK on Bainbridge Island. And if tennis isn't your sport, bring your favorite sports ball. There is a great basketball court and huge fields to play soccer and baseball. And if that's not enough, there are paths for bike riding, horseback riding, and roller skating. When you're ready to relax, enjoy the gazebo overlooking the duck pond or play a board game under the covered picnic area.

This park is incredible!

BEFORE YOU GO
●Bring your favorite sports equipment, bikes or
  board games. (If you don't own tennis rackets, check
  your local thrift store for great bargains.)
●Bring a picnic lunch or snacks and water.
●Bring day-old bread to feed the ducks.

ON THE WAY
●Watch for the totem pole on the west side
  of the Agate Pass Bridge. What animals
  can your children recognize?

HELPFUL INFORMATION
●Battlepoint Park is located on Bainbridge Island
●Take Highway 3 to Highway 305S (Poulsbo exit).
  Continue on Highway 305S through Poulsbo across the
  Agate Pass Bridge. Turn right on Day Road (the first
  light). Follow the road to the left as it turns into Miller
  Road. Continue on Miller Road and turn right on Arrow
  Point Drive. The park is on the left side.
●Battlepoint park is open year round, dawn to dusk.

MAKING MEMORIES
Play a game of Tennis Conversation together. Sit in a circle or in chairs
opposite each other. Toss around a dozen balls, but tell everyone to hold
them in their laps. After all the balls are gone talk about how the game
isn't much fun unless the balls are tossed back. Explain that conversation
is when people toss their ideas back and forth. Practice "tossing" words
back and forth. As you throw or roll the ball say, "What did you like best
at the park?" The reply must be a sentence. ("At the park, I liked playing
on the swings the best.") Encourage everyone to share ideas.

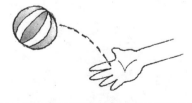

FABULOUS
MUSEUMS

TINY AND TERRIFIC

All kids are giants in this world. Come and see tiny pianos, tiny pots and pans and tiny toys at LITTLE HABITATS. This unique, Victorian house nestled in the woods of Port Orchard has over 2600 square feet of miniatures. Your children will be amazed and delighted with the Museum of Playtimes Past and Present. Can they find the tiny money tree? When they see Hairpin Hill, can they find the house that looks like Little Habitats? (It's only 2 inches tall!) On the way back, drive by LAZY R RANCH to see the exotic birds outside.

BEFORE YOU GO
●Bring a magnifying glass, if you have one.

ON THE WAY
●Have your children take turns sharing adventures they would have if they were the size of your thumb.

HELPFUL INFORMATION
●Little Habitats is located at 3238 Locker Road SE in Port Orchard.
●Take Highway 3 to Gorst. Follow the signs to Highway 16E (Tacoma) and take the Sedgwick exit. Go left off the freeway onto Sedgwick Road. Travel 3.5 miles and turn left on Locker Road and drive 1 mile. Little Habitats is on the left. (360) 871-1100
●Little Habitats is open Monday - Friday, 10 am - 5 pm; Saturday, 10 am - 4 pm.
●Admission: adults - $1.00; children under 6 are FREE.
●Lazy R Ranch is located at 3829 Locker Road.

MAKING MEMORIES

Your children will enjoy building a tasty graham cracker village. What you'll need:

> Graham crackers
> vanilla frosting
> gumdrops, Lifesavers, chocolate chips,
> licorice strings, decorating sprinkles,
> raisins, almonds, coconut, marshmallows
> empty individual milk cartons or
> half-pint cream cartons

Break the graham crackers into squares. Using the frosting, cement graham crackers to the sides of an individual milk carton. (Older kids can try building without this frame help.) Make different shaped buildings: barns, outhouses, stores, churches, schools, etc. Decorate with items you have collected. Lifesavers stacked can be a chimney, marshmallows in chimneys can be smoke or coconut can be snow. Have fun with your imagination. Add Lego men or toy cars to create your village. Have your children eat it before it gets too "played with" and is not edible.

GET YOUR HANDS IN IT

The MARINE SCIENCE CENTER in Poulsbo features a hands-on look at life in the waters of Puget Sound. Your children are encouraged to touch live sea creatures, view microscopic plankton and life-in-the-sediment exhibits, play computer games and enjoy other great displays about marine environments and water conservation. On Wednesdays at 11 am, sea stories are read. Come at noon on Thursdays and Saturdays or Sundays at 2 pm, to watch the sea creatures have lunch. Pick up a copy of the "Wonder of Puget Sound," a fun activity to do at home. Afterwards, walk down the street to SLUYS BAKERY for a delicious doughnut.

BEFORE YOU GO
- Be the "Water Patrol" and check for leaky faucets at your house.
- Look at your phone book map. What stream is located closest to your home?

ON THE WAY
- Talk about ways your family can save water at home. (Turn off the water while you brush your teeth, take showers instead of baths and keep cold water ready in the refrigerator.)

HELPFUL INFORMATION
- The Marine Science Center is located at 18743 NE Front Street in Poulsbo.
- Take Highway 3 to the Finn Hill exit. Turn right on Lindvig Way/Front Street and follow it into Old Poulsbo. Travel down Front Street past the stores. The Marine Science Center is on the right before you travel up the hill; parking is in front.
- The Marine Science Center is open Tuesday - Saturday, 10 am - 4 pm; Sunday, 12 pm - 4 pm. (360) 779-5549
- Admission: adults - $2.00; ages 2-12, 65 and older - $1.00; families $5.00.
- The third Tuesday of every month is FREE.
- Sluys Bakery is at 18924 Front Street, one block down.

MAKING MEMORIES

Make some hands for your punch. Fill two disposable latex gloves with water and put them in the freezer until frozen. After they are frozen cut the glove off and carefully rinse the ice hands. Put them in your punch bowl for "hands-in" fun.

UNDERSEA MYSTERIES

Experience the aura of the undersea world at the NAVAL UNDERSEA MUSEUM in Keyport. This museum is full of hands-on interactive displays complete with audio and visual effects. Go through a realistic cave to begin your adventure. See displays of undersea equipment and naval ships. View a jellyfish with a microscope and hear a grey whale in the ocean environment exhibits. How long can your children hold their breath? Touch real torpedoes and for extra fun play with the gyro wheel. Can you find the kidZibits? This place is great fun!!

BEFORE YOU GO

●Check a map to find where Keyport is located.
●Did you know Keyport was named because it was going to be a very busy "key to the port"?

ON THE WAY

●Have your children practice holding their breath. They can hold it as you wait for a stop light or as you go from one intersection to another.
●Did you know a sperm whale can hold its breath for two hours?
●Talk about what life is like in a submarine.

HELPFUL INFORMATION

●Naval Undersea Museum is located outside the Keyport gate.
●Take Highway 3 to the Keyport exit (Hwy 308). Go east on Highway 308 towards Keyport. Follow signs to the Naval Undersea Museum. (360) 396-4148
●The museum is open May - September, daily, 10 am - 4 pm; October - April, Wednesday - Monday, 10 am - 4 pm (closed Tuesday).
●Admission is FREE; donations are accepted.
●Docents are available to guide you through the museum or you can go by yourself.

MAKING MEMORIES

Use an appliance box to create a mini submarine for your children to play in. What you'll need:
    Appliance or large furniture box
    paint, pictures of fish, flashlights

First cut a hole in the back of the box to get in and out. Next paint the inside a dark blue or black. Cut out portholes for viewing and cover with plastic wrap. Draw pictures of marine plants and animals on the outside of the box. Hang fish pictures in front of the windows. Stock the submarine with tubes, lights, and gauges for an authentic look. You may even want to supply a flashlight to help your children imagine what it would be like under the sea in a sub. Dive!!!!

TWO TREASURES IN PORT GAMBLE

Up north in Port Gamble are two great adventures in one building. THE PORT GAMBLE COUNTRY STORE is filled with old-time toys. Watch the steamboat go around, dig in the treasure chest, and play the hurdy gurdy. The store is also well known for its clam chowder and yummy waffle cones. Head upstairs to see the largest sea shell collection in the United States at the OF SEA AND SHORE MUSEUM. It has scallops, abalones, conchs, horned helmets and much more. Find a Puget Sound king crab, a rib of a gray whale and a preserved baby hammerhead shark. This will be a favorite place for your family!

BEFORE YOU GO
●Bring some shells you might have at home to identify.

ON THE WAY
●Can your children say "She sells seashells by the seashore"? or "The Sheik's sixth sheep was sick"?
●Enjoy the drive into historic Port Gamble. Can your children find the Drew House?

HELPFUL INFORMATION
●Port Gamble Country Store and Of Sea and Shore Museum are located on Rainer Avenue in Port Gamble.
●Take Highway 3 towards Hood Canal Bridge. At the Bridge, Highway 3 turns into Highway 104. Continue past the bridge (do not cross it) on Highway 104E. Port Gamble is about a mile farther. Watch for museum signs.
●Port Gamble Country Store is open September - March, daily, 8 am - 5 pm; April - August, daily, 7 am - 7 pm. (360) 297-7636
●Of Sea & Shore museum is open September - May 30, Saturday and Sunday, 11 am - 4 pm; June - August, Tuesday - Sunday, 11 am - 4 pm. (360) 297-2426
●Admission to the museum is FREE; donations are accepted.

MAKING MEMORIES

Start a family shell collection. A pretty bottle is a nice way to display your treasures.

AHOY THERE, MATE

Imagine life in the Navy. The BREMERTON
NAVAL MUSEUM gives an up-close look at life on
the sea, important moments for the Navy and the
history of the Naval Shipyard. Your children can
grab hold of the captains steering wheel and
steer the boat to safety. Be sure to see the
Japanese sword collections, a real mine and the
Russian uniforms. Can your children find the
BIG E? If they're sure-fire ship mates, head on
down to the USS TURNER JOY. This Forrest
Sherman-class destroyer is open daily, May
through October for public tours.

BEFORE YOU GO
• Check a map to find the Port of Bremerton. Have your children trace the path a boat would take from the Pacific Ocean to Bremerton.

ON THE WAY
• Talk about why we have a Navy. Brainstorm people you know who serve in the Navy, talk about the job they do.

HELPFUL INFORMATION
• The Naval Museum and USS Turner Joy are located along the Bremerton waterfront.
• Take Highway 3 to Highway 303S/Waaga Way exit toward Bremerton. Waaga Way turns into Wheaton Way which turns into Warren Avenue. After you cross Warren Avenue Bridge, turn left on 11th Street. Follow 11th Street until it turns into Washington Street. The museum is on the left at 130 Washington Street.
• Parking is FREE along the street.
• The Naval Museum is open Monday - Saturday, 10 am - 5 pm; Sunday, 1 pm - 5 pm. (360) 479-7447
• Admission is FREE; donations are accepted.
• USS Turner Joy is at the north end of the Bremerton Boardwalk. Tickets are purchased at the Ship's Store and Gift Shop on the Boardwalk. (360) 792-2457
• USS Turner Joy is open May 15 - October 1, 10 am to dusk.
• Admission: adults - $5.00; children (5-12) $3.00.

MAKING MEMORIES

Your children can set the ocean in motion, inside a bottle. What you'll need:
   a clear plastic bottle with a lid
   water, cooking oil, blue food coloring, small toy boat
Fill the bottle halfway with water, add blue food coloring and fill the rest of the bottle with oil. Make sure the mixture reaches the very top of the bottle. Add the toy boat, screw the lid on tightly and wipe away any oil from the sides of the bottle. Now imagine navigating through high seas.

OTHER PLACES
TO GO

KAYAKING FOR KIDS

Have your children ever tried kayaking?
This family-fun sport is waiting for you in
the calm waters of Poulsbo's Liberty Bay.
OLYMPIC OUTDOOR CENTER can outfit your
family and get you safely started on this marine
adventure. As you navigate the bay, watch for
harbor seals and bald eagles. They're out there!
As you float have your children close their
eyes and listen to all the different sounds.
Finish off your adventure with a milk shake
at the old-fashioned soda counter in the
POULSBO DRUG STORE.

BEFORE YOU GO
- Wear layered clothes.
- Bring sunscreen.

ON THE WAY
- Brainstorm items that float. What makes them float?
- Did you know that when you're in a kayak, you sit at or below the water line, making the center of gravity so low that it would take a huge force to knock you over?

HELPFUL INFORMATION
- Olympic Outdoor Center is located at 18971 Front Street in Poulsbo.
- Take Highway 3 to the Finn Hill exit. Turn right onto Lindvig Way/Front Street and follow it into Old Poulsbo. Olympic Outdoor Center is on the right.
- Olympic Outdoor Center is open in the summer, Monday - Saturday, 9 am - 8 pm; Sunday, 10 am - 6 pm; in the winter, daily, 9 am - 6 pm.
- Kayaking rental fees are $10.00 per hour and up. Included are a boat, paddles, lifejackets and other equipment.
- They have single, double and triple kayaks, as well as canoes.
- For more information and reservations call (360) 697-6095.
- Poulsbo Drug Store is located at 18911 Front Street. (360) 779-2737

MAKING MEMORIES

Float a candle or flower in a fairly flat bowl as a table centerpiece.

A BUCKET OF BALLS

Rain or shine, day or night, summer or winter, your family can have this adventure anytime! Imagine golfing with Tiger Woods at the National Championships...it all could start with a bucket of balls at NORTHWEST GOLF RANGE. Just how far can your children hit that ball? When you're done, go to DAILY STOP, the only corner store that still sells candy for a penny. Give the kids 50 cents each; you'll be shocked at how much candy they come back with!

BEFORE YOU GO
●Have your chidren do stretching exercises and practice their golf swing.

ON THE WAY
●Did you know the first golf balls were handmade out of feathers covered with leather? Now they are machine made by winding rubber threads around a core. The cover is made from the gum of the bully tree. The little bumps or dimples make the balls go faster.

HELPFUL INFORMATION
●Northwest Golf Range is located at 368 NE Waaga Way.
●Take Highway 3 to Highway 303S exit/Waaga Way.
  Take Waaga Way east toward Bremerton. Just after the Central Valley exit, turn LEFT into Northwest Golf Range. (360) 692-6828
●NW Golf Range is open daily, 9 am - 10 pm. (360)
●Prices are: $2.00 - children's bucket of balls;
  $3.00 - small bucket; $4.00 - large bucket.
●Clubs can be borrowed.
●Daily Stop is at 9730 Brownsville Highway. (360) 692-2073
●To get to Daily Stop, continue east.on Waaga Way.
  Take the next left on Gluds Pond Road. Go one block and turn left onto the Brownsville Highway.
  Daily Stop is .7 mile on the right.

MAKING MEMORIES
Draw a "holey" picture with a golf tee. What you'll need:
  a golf tee
  Paper (construction paper is good)
  pencil
Have your children draw a simple picture on the
paper; try a tree. They can set it down on a rug or
in the grass. Take the golf tee and poke holes along
the lines of the picture. When they're done place a
light behind it or hang it in the window to see a great scene.

COUPON BOWLING
MORNING OR NIGHT

Get up early one morning and start your day at the bowling alley. With coupons, ALL STAR LANES in Silverdale will serve you breakfast for only a buck. Then your chidren can enjoy bowling a game or two. If an early morning is not your idea of fun, then how about midnight bowling? You can use coupons for late night bowling and bring your own hot chocolate. The kids will think it's fun to be up at midnight when nobody is around. Be sure to ask for bumper guards; it makes bowling MUCH more enjoyable for beginning bowlers.

BEFORE YOU GO
●Get a good night's sleep.
●Get your bowling coupons.

ON THE WAY
●Talk about the difference between a strike and a spare.

HELPFUL INFORMATION
●All Star Lanes is located at 10710 Silverdale Way NW
in Silverdale.
●Take Highway 3 to the Highway 303S/Silverdale exit. Go
south on Kitsap Mall Boulevard. Take the first left on
Randall Way. Follow Randall Way to the end of the road
and turn right onto Silverdale Way. All Star Lanes is
on the left. (360) 692-5760
●Restaurant hours: Sunday - Thursday, 6 am - 9 pm;
Friday and Saturday, 6 am - 10 pm.
●Each person needs their OWN coupon.
●Breakfast coupon is on the back of Fred Meyer receipts
and is for one egg (fried), hash browns and toast
(no substitutions, please). This breakfast coupon is good
Monday - Friday, 6 am - 11 am.
●Midnight bowling coupons are on the back of Silverdale
Safeway receipts. This coupon offers 2 free games with
2 paid games, including shoes; the coupon is valid
Sunday - Thursday evenings, 9 pm - 2 am.
●It is recommended you call ahead for lane availability.

MAKING MEMORIES
For more bowling fun do candlelight bowling with your children.
What you'll need:
   10 votive candles
Place the votive candles in a bowling configuration.
Take turns blowing out the "candle pins". Vary the
distance away for different degrees of difficulty.
Your children can add their own scores.
(This is supervised activity.)

MY, OH MY, WHAT DELICIOUS PIE!!!

What is your favorite kind of pie? Chocolate
Cream, Blackberry, Lemon Meringue, Cherry
or just good old-fashioned Dutch Apple?
CHIMACUM CAFE in Chimacum makes 20
varieties of fresh pies every day. Give yourself
a break from your routine and enjoy the time
together as you take a drive in the country.
Watch for the Egg & I Rd, off of Highway 19 on
the left. This road was made famous with Betty
McDonald's Ma & Pa Kettle Book, "The Egg & I."

BEFORE YOU GO
●Bring along paper and crayons.

ON THE WAY
●Your children can pass the time playing a pie game. Have them draw five circles and color them their favorite pie colors. They can cut up their pies to serve 2, 4, 6, 8 & 10 people. (Did they know they were drawing fractions?)

HELPFUL INFORMATION
●Take Highway 3 to Highway 104W across the Hood Canal Bridge. Travel 4.7 miles and turn right on Highway 19N (to Chimacum). Just 4.6 miles on the left will be the Egg & I Rd. Continue on 4.5 more miles to the cafe on the left.
●Chimacum Cafe is open daily, 6 am - 9 pm. (360) 732-4631

MAKING MEMORIES

Pies don't have to be just for dessert. Try one for dinner. Here's a recipe for Itty Bitty Chicken Pot Pies. What you'll need:
  2 pre-made pie crusts
  2 cups cubed chicken
  4 to 5 cups vegetables chopped small (carrots,
    peas, onions, potatoes and celery)
  1 can each cream of chicken and cream of celery soup
  $\frac{1}{2}$ cup milk, spices (salt & pepper, 1 tsp. sage,
    pinch of tarragon or marjoram)
  2 TBS. butter

Roll out pie crusts, making them smooth and larger in diameter. Use a cup to cut 24 circles out of the two crusts. In a greased muffin tin place one circle in each muffin cup. Mix together the rest of the ingredients, except butter. Fill each muffin cup with this mixture. Put a dab of butter in each cup. Top with another circle crust and pinch edges together. Bake at 350° for 50 minutes.

DRIVE-IN DRAMAS

When was the last time your family went to
a drive-in movie? Chances are it's been a
while. Experience a unique evening watching a
movie the old-fashioned way at Bremerton's
RODEO DRIVE-IN. Just a short drive outside
Bremerton, this rural outdoor theatre is one
family fun activity perfect for those
summer memories.

BEFORE YOU GO
●Bring popcorn and some snacks.
●Bring comfy pillows and blankets.

ON THE WAY
●Talk about what movies you have seen lately.
  Which was a favorite and why?

HELPFUL INFORMATION
●Rodeo Drive-in is located between Bremerton and Belfair.
●Take Highway 3 to Gorst, staying in the right lane.
  At Gorst follow signs to Bremerton Nt'l Airport (Hwy 3S)
  and Belfair. Drive 2.5 miles on Highway 3S. The movie
  theatre is on the right.
●Rodeo drive-in is open in the spring and summer.
●For more information call (360) 698-6030.

MAKING MEMORIES

Help your children make their own movie.
With a flip-book, their drawings
really come alive. What you'll need:
    small unruled pad of white paper
    (a 5x7 inch pad is good)
    pencil or pen
    masking tape

Reinforce the binding of the pad with a
piece of masking tape. Go to the last
page of the pad and make your first
drawing. Keep your drawings to the
bottom two-thirds of the paper because
those drawn higher up won't be seen.
Keep it simple, try drawing a ball. Turn to the next page. You should be
able to see your first drawing through the page. Use that drawing as your
guide. The second drawing should look almost the same as the first, but
with a small difference (maybe to the left a little). Continue this way until
you make thirty or forty drawings. (Twenty-four drawings make about one
second of viewing time.) To watch your drawing move, hold the binding of
the pad with your right hand, and flip through the pages with your left
hand. Try flipping faster and slower. Try changing the color or size of
your object. Try drawing a person running.

FIND THE BOOKS

At KITSAP REGIONAL LIBRARY you can hunt
for all kinds of books. These books are treasures
waiting to be discovered. Enjoy books on every
subject imaginable. What topics fascinate your
children? What do they want to learn about?
With nine branches to visit, the library can help
you make reading fun for the whole family.
The library even has storytimes for your younger
children. As you hunt together, your world
will open up. From astronomy to zoology.....the
choices are unlimited!

BEFORE YOU GO
● If you don't have a library card, bring proof of address in order to apply for one.
● Time flies in the library, so plan ahead for little ones who might need a snack in the car.

ON THE WAY
● Talk about the difference between a library and a bookstore. What are some library rules you know?

HELPFUL INFORMATION
● Library branches worth checking out include:
  -CENTRAL BRANCH: (1301 Sylvan Way) is open Monday - Thursday, 9:30 am - 9 pm; Friday and Saturday, 9:30 am - 5:30 pm; Sunday, 12:30 pm - 5:30 pm. (360) 377-7601
  -BAINBRIDGE ISLAND BRANCH: (1270 Madison N) is open Monday, Tuesday, Thursday, Friday, and Saturday, 10 am - 5:30 pm; Wednesday 10 am - 8:30 pm; Sunday 1 pm - 5 pm. (206) 842-4162
  -DOWNTOWN BREMERTON BRANCH: (612- 5th Street) is open Monday - Friday, 10 am - 5:30 pm. (360) 377-3955
  -KINGSTON BRANCH: (Community Center) is open Tuesday, Thursday, 1 pm - 8:30 pm; Wednesday, Friday, 1 pm - 8:30 pm; Saturday, 1 pm - 5:30 pm. (360) 297-3330
  -LITTLE BOSTON BRANCH: (31980 Little Boston Road NE) is open Monday, Wednesday, 1 pm - 5:30 pm; Tuesday, Thursday, 1 pm - 8:30 pm; Saturday, 9 am - 1 pm. (360) 297-2670
  -POULSBO BRANCH: (700 NE Lincoln Street) is open Monday, Tuesday, 10 am - 8:30 pm; Wednesday, 1 pm - 8:30 pm; Thursday, 1 pm - 5:30 pm; Friday, Saturday, 10 am - 5:30 pm; Sunday, 1 pm - 5 pm. (360) 779-2915
  -SILVERDALE BRANCH: (3450 NW Carlton Street) is open Monday, Wednesday, 10 am - 8:30 pm; Tuesday, Friday, 10 am - 5:30 pm; Thursday, 1 pm - 5:30 pm; Saturday, 10 am - 5:30 pm. (360) 692-2779
  -MANCHESTER BRANCH: (8067 East Main Street) is open Tuesday, Saturday, 10 am - 5:30 pm; Wednesday, Thursday, 1 pm - 8:30 pm; Friday, 1 pm - 5:30 pm. (360) 871-3921
  -DOWNTOWN PORT ORCHARD BRANCH: (87 Sidney Avenue) is open Monday, Wednesday, 10 am - 8:30 pm; Tuesday, 1 pm - 8:30 pm; Thursday, Friday, Saturday, 10 am - 5:30 pm; Sunday, 1 pm - 5 pm. (360) 876-2224

MAKING MEMORIES
Snuggle up together with a good book.

DANCING BRUSH

Create memorable gifts with your family as you spend a pleasant afternoon or evening at the DANCING BRUSH in Poulsbo. This new contemporary shop is filled with ceramic items just waiting for your creative touch. Treasured gifts can be made for special people. Artists young and old will enjoy designing, painting or stenciling their masterpieces. After firing, your finished artwork is displayed in the front window until you pick it up.

BEFORE YOU GO
●Think about who would enjoy your handmade gifts.

ON THE WAY
●Talk about handmade gifts. What makes them so special?

HELPFUL INFORMATION
●The Dancing Brush is located at 18846 Front Street
in Poulsbo.
●Take Highway 3 to the Finn Hill exit. Turn right onto
Lindvig Way/Front Street and follow it into Old Poulsbo.
The Dancing Brush is on the left. (360) 598-3800
●The Dancing Brush is open daily, 10 am-9 pm
(8 pm is the last starting time).
●Costs include ceramic pieces ranging from $5-$30 each
and a $6.00 hourly fee which covers firing, any colored
glazes and use of stamps, stencils and sponges.
Many idea cards are available.
●Ceramic items are available for pickup three to
five days later, or can be mailed.

MAKING MEMORIES

Make handmade gift wrap to wrap your treasures in. What you'll need:
    butcher paper or brown bags (inside out)
    tempera paints, marbles
Cover the marble with paint. Place the marble on the paper. Carefully roll
the marble on the paper. Use different colors for crazy designs.

ROLLING AROUND
THE RINK

Rain or shine you can take your kids to Bremerton's SKATELAND for roller-skating fun. Wednesday morning is a great time to bring the preschoolers, strollers and all. The afternoon session on Wednesday is perfect for the school age group. Saturday and Sunday there are two sessions for kids needing to burn some energy. Join in the Hokey Poky, try to Shoot the Duck and listen for lucky number winners. Skating in the evening is fun with music choices for everyone throughout the week. For those enthusiastic skaters there are lessons to teach one foot balance, skating backwards, crossovers, jumps and spins. What fun!!

BEFORE YOU GO
● Bring a snack or water.
● Bring your own roller blades.

ON THE WAY
● As you drive to the roller rink, have your children look at all the wheels rolling around you. Can they count how many they see along the way?

HELPFUL INFORMATION
● Bremerton Skateland is located at 1740 NE Fuson Road in Bremerton.
● Take Highway 3 to Highway 303S exit/Waaga Way toward Bremerton. Waaga Way turns into Wheaton Way. Watch for their sign between McWilliams Road and Riddell Road on the left.
● Some evenings that are worth checking include:
 - Monday: Christian "Pop" music nite; 6:30 pm - 9 pm
 - Tuesday and Thursday: PTA nite; 6:30 pm - 8:30 pm
 - Wednesday: BUCK nite; 7 pm - 9:30 pm
 - Friday and Saturday: Late nite; 7 pm - 11 pm
 - Sunday: Adult nite; 7 pm - 9:30 pm
● Costs range from $1.00 to $5.00.
● For more information call (360) 479-7655.

MAKING MEMORIES

After all that roller-skating, give each other a foot rub!

MEET ANIMAL MOVIE STARS

Your children can meet Hollywood movie stars in nearby Sequim. This animal adventure is waiting for you at the OLYMPIC GAME FARM. Experience wild animals at close range: bears playing, llamas grazing and buffaloes slobbering at your windows. A 45-minute driving tour will introduce you to animal movie stars, help you learn about endangered species and give you great photo opportunities. In the summer you can take a guided walking tour and see lions, tigers and bears! Stop at the petting farm and then enjoy a picnic at the observation tower before heading home.

BEFORE YOU GO
●Bring a lunch or snacks and water.
●Bring a camera.
●Bring paper and crayons for the drive.

ON THE WAY
●Brainstorm as many endangered animals as you can.
●Have your children draw silly animals (head of a lion, body of a horse, etc.).

HELPFUL INFORMATION
●The Olympic Game Farm is located at 1423 Ward Road in Sequim.
●Take Highway 3N to Highway 104W across the Hood Canal Bridge. Continue on to Highway 104W toward Port Angeles. After entering Sequim turn right on Sequim Avenue. Go 2½ miles and turn left on Woodcock Road. After crossing the Dungeness River, take a right on Ward Road. 1-800-778-4295
●The Olympic Game Farm is open daily, 9 am - 4 pm.
●Admission: adults -$6.00; ages 5-12, 65 and older -$5.00; children under 4 are FREE, cash is preferred.

MAKING MEMORIES

Hunt down a video starring one of the animals you've seen or filmed at the Olympic Game Farm. Choose from: "Never Cry Wolf," "Kid Colter," "The Incredible Journey," "Those Calloways, " Nikki, Wild Dog of the North," and "Life and Times of Grizzly Adams." Eat animal crackers together as you watch your video.

WALK IN THE WILD AND SWIM IN THE SEA

Are your children getting a little wild? Restless with all the time indoors? Take them out for a walk in the wild at the HOOD CANAL/THELER WETLANDS in Belfair. Your children will burn energy and have a good time while they explore great trails. Floating boardwalks go over swamps and paths lead to the meadow. If you walk quietly you can see frogs, mallards, river otters and all kinds of birds. Along the trail, stop in at the Exhibitory building for hands-on displays. The easy trail is 3.8 miles and takes about 1.5 hours to walk; just long enough for you to enjoy this wild time outdoors. Then go play in the warm waters of TWANOH STATE PARK. For extra fun, your children can make a unique beach souvenir with plaster of Paris in the sand.

BEFORE YOU GO
● Pack for your family; include extra clothing, beach chairs, towels, binoculars, old tennis shoes and sunscreen.
● Bring plaster of Paris to make a beach souvenir.

ON THE WAY
● Enjoy the scenery as it changes from urban to rural to urban. Did you see the treatment plant, the drive-in theatre and the airport?
● Did you know that Belfair sells more Christmas trees than anywhere else in the U.S.?

HELPFUL INFORMATION
● Hood Canal/Theler Wetland is located in Belfair.
● Take Highway 3 to Gorst, staying in the right lane. At Gorst, follow signs to Bremerton Nt'l. Airport (3S) and Belfair. Continue 8.5 miles into Belfair to the Mary E. Theler Community Center on the right. The trailhead is located south of the building. (360) 275-4898
● The Hood Canal/Theler Wetlands is open daily, dawn to dusk.
● Admission is FREE; donations are accepted.
● Twanoh State Park is $8\frac{1}{2}$ miles southwest on Highway 106. Turn right out of the Center and right again on Highway 106W. Twanoh State Park has a wading pool, swimming area, horseshoe pits and picnic sites.

MAKING MEMORIES
Create a fun beach souvenir. What you'll need:
   Plaster of Paris (find it at hardware or craft stores)
   Empty coffee can or plastic container
   Stirring stick and paper clips
   Shells, driftwood, or other beach treasures

Make a 4-inch hole in the sand and press shells or driftwood treasures into the sides of the hole (with the shell's "pretty" sides facing the sand). Following the directions on the box, mix plaster of Paris with fresh water in a disposable container, using the stirring stick. Fill your hole with the plaster and let it set (1 to 1 $\frac{1}{2}$ hours). Dispose of leftover plaster properly.

GO BACKWARD
IN TIME

Go backward in time on this adventure. Step onto
the historic Mosquito Fleet's FOOT FERRY at the
Bremerton waterfront and travel old-time style
across the Sinclair Inlet to the quaint town of
Port Orchard. Once you've landed, stroll over to
Bay Street to see the OLDE CENTRAL ANTIQUE
MALL. You'll find collectibles and treasures of
long ago. Stop at MYHRE'S CAFE to look at all
the old photos and have an old-fashioned milk
shake. End your backwards adventure by planning
a backwards day.

BEFORE YOU GO
•Wear layered clothes.

ON THE WAY
•As you travel across the bay on the foot ferry, do you see the many Navy ships?

HELPFUL INFORMATION
•Catch the foot ferry at the Bremerton Waterfront.
•Take Highway 3 to Highway 303S exit/Waaga Way toward Bremerton. Waaga Way turns into Wheaton Way which turns into Warren Avenue. After crossing Warren Avenue Bridge turn left on 11th Street. Follow signs to the ferry.
•The foot ferry boats leave every 30 minutes, 6:30 am to 12:30 am. (360) 876-2300
•You can find FREE parking along the street. Pay parking lots are also available.
•This 10-minute ride is $1.00 for adults, 50¢ for children 6-11. Rides are FREE on Saturdays and Sundays, May - October.
•Olde Central Antique Mall is located at 801 Bay Street in Port Orchard. Sidney Village, The Side Door Mall and Ma Barker's may be places you'll want to visit too.
•Myhre's Cafe is located at 739 Bay Street.

MAKING MEMORIES

Have a backwards day. Everything is done backwards. Start the day with a bedtime story and some dessert. Try backwards clothing, a backwards hairdo and walking backwards. Can you write backwards too? End the crazy day with pancakes shaped like initials. How far backwards you go is limited only by your family's imagination.

IT'S THYME FOR HERBS

Kids can have lots of fun discovering smells and tastes at SILVER BAY HERB FARM. Rosemary, lavender, sage and lemon balm mint are just a few of the herbs they can find in the farm's garden. Let your children taste the fennel growing there; it has a licorice flavor. They can wander the garden paths, look for the compost pile and find the rocks which label the herbs. If you're lucky you'll see Elvis Preuss(ly), the owner's friendly dog, wandering the garden.

BEFORE YOU GO

●Look through your kitchen cupboard and see what herbs you have. Help your children write them down on a piece of paper and tape a sample next to it. Take it to the Herb Farm and compare them with fresh herbs.

●Bring Elvis a dog biscuit.

ON THE WAY

●Did you know herbs have been grown for thousands of years, and some are even mentioned in the Bible? (Cinnamon, Mint, Cumin, Mustard and Caraway Seeds.)

●For extra fun, stop over the bridge, as you drive down the Herb Farm driveway, and see minnows in the water below.

HELPFUL INFORMATION

●Silver Bay Herb Farm is located at 9151 Tracyton Boulevard in Silverdale.

●Take Highway 3 to Highway 303S exit/Waaga Way. Take Waaga Way to Ridgetop Boulevard exit. Go west on Ridgetop Boulevard and left at the first light, Myhre. Continue on Myhre, it turns into Tracyton Boulevard. (360) 692-1340

●The farm is open mid March - late December, Thursday - Sunday, 10 am - 5 pm or by appointment.

MAKING MEMORIES

Make some lemonade with some lemon balm. What you'll need:
  hot water
  lemon balm
  ice
  sugar and lemon juice to taste
Wash and cut up or tear 1 cup of lemon balm leaves. Pour 1 quart of boiling water over the leaves and let them "steep" for 5-10 minutes. Strain the liquid, and let it cool. Squeeze fresh lemon juice and add sugar to taste. Pour over ice cubes for a delicious glass of lemonade.

GROWING AT THE CHILDREN'S GARDEN

There are no plants growing at the CHILDREN'S GARDEN in Silverdale. The things growing there are minds and imaginations. Your children can play with high quality toys as you explore the store together. Yes, this store is filled with educationally sound, developmentally appropriate materials for children of all ages, and it's a really fun place to visit! There are six play stations for your children, even one for the baby. The multi-purpose room is used for story-telling, arts & crafts and play groups. Sign your children up for a fun science class with hands-on experiments or participate in the summer reading club, the American Girls Tea or a seasonal party. This place makes learning FUN!!

BEFORE YOU GO
●Have your children each pick a favorite toy at home.

ON THE WAY
●Talk about what makes a toy fun. Ask some questions about your children's toy. (Does it teach important skills? Does it support our values? How long will it last? How long is it really played with each week?)

HELPFUL INFORMATION
●Children's Garden is located at 10876 Myhre Place in Silverdale.
●Take Highway 3 to Highway 303S/Silverdale exit. Go south on Kitsap Mall Boulevard. Take the first left on Randall Way. Travel 3 blocks and turn left on Myhre Place NW. (360) 698-7581
●Children's Garden is open Monday - Friday, 9 am - 9 pm; Saturday, 9 am - 7 pm; Sunday, 10 am - 6 pm.

MAKING MEMORIES

Make old pennies look new with this fun "penny bath" science experiment you can do with your children. What you'll need:
  old pennies
  4 TBS. vinegar
  1 tsp. salt
  vegetable oil
  soft cloth
Mix vinegar and salt in a small mixing bowl. Have your children drop the pennies in the solution and stir them with a wooden spoon. Watch what happens. After the pennies are clean polish them with a soft cloth and a drop of vegetable oil to make them shine.

SWIMMING ANYONE?

Splish, splash, drip, drop. Water, water, everywhere around us. Unfortunately, most of it's just too cold to swim in. So all over the county, indoor SWIMMING POOLS are available for your family's enjoyment. You'll find indoor pools on Bainbridge Island, on Bangor base, in Poulsbo and in Port Orchard. There are three in Bremerton; one near the fairgrounds, one near the hospital and one at the Puget Sound Naval Shipyard. For those who want to bask in the sun there is one outdoor pool for you, open in the summer only, at Lange's Ranch in Keyport. Explore them all or find the pool closest to you and enjoy this wet adventure together.

BEFORE YOU GO
●Call for individual hours and activities.
●Bring "on the way home" raisin snacks for exhausted wrinkled swimmers.

ON THE WAY
●Did you know your body is made up of two-thirds water? No wonder you can float so easily! Talk about other things that float.

HELPFUL INFORMATION
●Each pool has different public swim hours and costs. Call for details. Flotation devices are usually not allowed.
●Season passes, and punch cards are at most pools.
●Ask about lessons and birthday party accommodations.
●Some pools that are worth checking out include:
-RAY WILLIAMSON MEMORIAL POOL: Madison Avenue NE and High School Road on Bainbridge Island. (206) 842-2302
-BANGOR POOL: Naval Submarine Base Bangor in Silverdale (Base access required). (360) 779-4817
-NORTH KITSAP COMMUNITY POOL: 1881 NE Hostmark in Poulsbo. (360) 598-1070
-OLYMPIC SWIM CENTER: Olympic High School, 7070 Stampede Boulevard in East Bremerton. (360) 692-3217
-GLEN JARSTAD AQUATIC CENTER: 50 Magnuson Way in Bremerton. (360) 478-5376
-PUGET SOUND NAVAL SHIPYARD POOL: Puget Sound Naval Shipyard in Bremerton (Base access required). (360) 476-2593
-SOUTH KITSAP POOL: South Kitsap High School, 425 Mitchell Avenue in Port Orchard. (360) 876-7385
-LANGE'S RANCH: 13913 S. Keyport Road in Keyport. (360) 779-4927

MAKING MEMORIES
Your children can make a song with tapped water. What you'll need:
    8 glass jars or glasses
    wooden spoon
Line up the glasses on a table. Fill each glass with equal and varying amounts of water (the first glass has the most water and the last glass has no water). Tap the rims gently with a spoon to play Twinkle, Twinkle, Little Star. (1-1-5-5-6-6-5, 4-4-3-3-2-2-1,5-5-4-4-3-3-2,5-5-4-4-3-3-2,1-1-5-5-6-6-5,4-4-3-3-2-2-1)

THE TROLL HAVEN

For a fun drive and a chance to see an unusual purple stone castle, wood-carved sculptures and a giant rocking chair, take a ride out to Gardiner to see the TROLL HAVEN. You'll see several houses, each creatively using trolls and other carved creatures. The carved troll fence posts are uniquely individual. Can you find the one picking his nose? After seeing these crazy sights backtrack to the RAILROAD PARK for a tasty treat of ice cream. The licorice flavor will turn your children's mouths black! Kids will have fun climbing on the 1950's cabooses and engine. They can even pull the steam whistle. This troll adventure is sure to be talked about for quite some time.

BEFORE YOU GO
●Bring pencil and paper for drawing on the way.

ON THE WAY
●Look for a green castle here in Kitsap county. You can see it as you drive toward the Hood Canal Bridge on Hwy 3. The castle is just 4 driveways north past Snider baseball park on the right.

●Have your children draw a castle to live in.

HELPFUL INFORMATION
●Troll Haven is located in Gardiner.

●Take Highway 3 to Highway 104W across the Hood Canal Bridge. Continue on Highway 104W to Highway 101N. Travel 8 more miles and turn right on Gardiner Beach Road (not Old Gardiner Rd). Go one block and then turn left on Old Gardiner Beach Road to the boat ramp. You will see signs to the Troll Haven.

●This is a private residence and a small community; please do not trespass.

●The Railroad Park is located on Highway 101. They have ice cream, candy, pizza and a deli. For more information call (360) 385-9490.

MAKING MEMORIES

Help your children make their own sculpture using soap. What you'll need:
   Ivory works well, because it is soft
   carving tools (spoon, fork, butter knife or plastic knife)
   paper and pencil

Trace the soap outline on paper. On that paper have your children draw a picture of what they want their soap carving to look like. Put the paper back on your soap and trace the outline of the carving with a pencil. They can use a knife to remove bits of soap a little at a time until they have the shape they want.
Gently rub the soap with a damp cloth for a smooth finish.

PLAY ALL OVER THE COUNTY

All over the county are incredible playing structures just waiting for your energetic kids. With over 40 elementary schools in Kitsap County there are many SCHOOL PLAYGROUNDS to explore FREE. Some boast loooong slides, others have colorful climbing structures, hopscotch, balance beams and covered play areas. There are schools that have tetherballs, big tires, monkey bars and even funnel ball equipment (that's where the ball goes in one basketball hoop but has the chance to come out of three different holes). Try to find the playground with the map of the United States, the sand box or the circular twisty slide.

BEFORE YOU GO
●Bring a lunch or snacks with water.
●Bring basketballs, soccer balls, Frisbees or jump ropes.
●Bring your camera for playground photos or a tape measure for slide measurements.
●Check your map for easier driving.

ON THE WAY
●Exercise your brain on the way with this brainteaser:
"A bus driver was going down the street. He went right past a stop sign without stopping. He turned left where there was a 'no left turn' sign. Then he turned the wrong way into a one-way street. And yet, he didn't break a single traffic law. Why not?"
Answer: It was his day off and he was walking.

HELPFUL INFORMATION
●Playgrounds that are worth checking out include:
-JOHNSTON BLAKELY ELEMENTARY; 4704 Blakely NE on Bainbridge
-SUQUAMISH ELEMENTARY; 18950 Park Avenue NE in Suquamish
-BREIDABLICK ELEMENTARY; 25142 Waghorn Road NW in Poulsbo
-RICHARD GORDON JR. ELEMENTARY; 26331 Barber Cut Off - Kingston
-HILDER PEARSON ELEMENTARY; 15650 Central Valley Road in Scandia
-COUGAR VALLEY ELEMENTARY; 13200 Olympic View Rd NW -Silverdale
-JACKSON PARK ELEMENTARY; 6200 Dowell Road in East Bremerton
-COTTONWOOD ELEMENTARY; 330 NE Foster Road in East Bremerton
-VIEW RIDGE ELEMENTARY; 3220 Wheaton Way in Bremerton
-WEST HILLS ELEMENTARY; 520 National Street in Bremerton
-EAST PORT ORCHARD ELEMENTARY; 1964 Hoover SE, in Port Orchard
-MANCHESTER ELEMENTARY; 1901 California in Port Orchard
-BURLEY-GLENWOOD ELEMENTARY; 100 SE Lakebay Blvd in Pt Orchard

---

MAKING MEMORIES

Create a display for your playground photos
(maybe a collage you can keep adding to).

FALL
ADVENTURES

BLACKBERRIES IN BREMERTON

Just when you think summer is over, along comes a wonderful opportunity for food and fun. The BLACKBERRY FESTIVAL is held on Labor Day weekend, at Bremerton's boardwalk, and celebrates the native blackberry. You'll find all kinds of blackberry treats to eat. Do some chalk art together and enjoy a ride on a pony or a train. Watch the bathtub races, or enjoy entertainment on the children's stage. This festival is a great way to end the summer.

BEFORE YOU GO
●Wear comfortable clothes, according to the weather.
●Bring blankets to sit on.
●Consider taking a shuttle available from Kitsap Transit for a more relaxing adventure.

ON THE WAY
●Did you know the blackberry is rich in vitamin C and potassium? The blacker the berry, the sweeter it is.
●Count how many bushes you see along the way.

HELPFUL INFORMATION
●The Blackberry Festival is held on the waterfront boardwalk in Bremerton.
●Take Highway 3 to Highway 303S exit/Waaga Way toward Bremerton. Waaga Way turns into Wheaton Way, which turns into Warren Avenue. After crossing the Warren Avenue Bridge turn left on 6th Street.
●The Blackberry Festival is usually held on Labor Day weekend.
●Admission is FREE; there can be optional expenses.
●Shuttles are available through Kitsap Transit. For more information call (360) 373-2877.

MAKING MEMORIES
Make a blackberry cobbler. What you'll need:
  4 - 6 cups washed blackberries
  1 cup flour
  ½ tsp. salt
  1 egg
  1 cup sugar, plus 2 TBS.
  ¾ tsp. baking powder
  cinnamon and nutmeg
  ½ cup oil

Spread blackberries in a 9x12 baking pan. Sprinkle with 2 TBS. sugar. Combine flour, salt, egg, sugar, and baking powder and crumble over berries. Sprinkle cinnamon and nutmeg on top. Cover with oil. Bake 40-50 minutes at 350°. Serve warm with vanilla ice-cream.

SCADS OF SILLY SCARECROWS

Guaranteed to be fun is the FALL FESTIVAL at VALLEY NURSERY in Poulsbo. Families, and especially children, are encouraged to participate in both the scarecrow contest and the veggie extravaganza in this annual event in October. Be creative and make a ballerina, a proper lady or a businessman scarecrow for prizes. In the Veggie extravaganza, your home-grown vegetables can compete for prizes, too. Bring in your BIG zucchinis or silly-looking potatoes. See giant pumpkins, grown all over the area by gardeners vying for the prize of "Grand Pumpkin." Be sure to take a look at all the birds near the barn and enjoy the FREE pressed cider and popcorn throughout the weekend.

BEFORE YOU GO

● Make your scarecrow at home or bring everything to assemble there. Use your imagination; heads can be made from stuffed pillowcases, plastic jugs, pumpkins, flower pots, shovels or old balls. Add details like gloves, boots, scarves, hats or jewelry.
● Call for rules and contest information.

ON THE WAY

● Talk about why farmers used scarecrows. Did you know 3,000 years ago Greeks carved wooden statues to frighten birds from their fields?
● What was the scarecrow in "The Wizard of Oz" missing?

HELPFUL INFORMATION

● Valley Nursery is located at 20882 Bond Road NE in Poulsbo.
● Take Highway 3 to 305S (Poulsbo exit). Continue on Highway 305S and go left at Bond Road (307N) Valley Nursery is on the right, one block down.
  Watch for the giant troll, ValNur, outside.
● The Festival usually is held in October. For more information call (360) 779-3806.
● Admission is FREE; there can be optional expenses.

MAKING MEMORIES
Dress up together and use your imagination for some silly fun.

A TRIP TO
A PUMPKIN FARM

Support our local farming families by buying
pumpkins right off the vine. There are many
pumpkin farms all over the county, making buying
a pumpkin a great fall adventure. One especially
fun farm is the WILLOWBROOK FARM on
Bainbridge Island. Every weekend in October this
working farm is opened up to the public. Bring the
family for fresh apple cider, taste all kinds of
apples and pick from eight different varieties of
pumpkins. Can your children find the white
pumpkin, the Cinderella pumpkin or the pumpkin
that looks like a zucchini? They can play in a
"fort" made from straw bales and enjoy seeing
miniature horses.

BEFORE YOU GO

- Wear comfortable layered clothing, according to the weather.
- Bring umbrellas if needed.
- Bring your camera for fun farm photos.

ON THE WAY

- As you drive count how many pumpkin decorations you see along the way. Did you know the biggest pumpkin grown in Washington was 612 pounds and grown in Chelan by Norman Gallagher?

HELPFUL INFORMATION

- Willowbook Farm is located at 12600 Miller Road NE on Bainbridge Island.
- Take Highway 3 to Highway 305S (Poulsbo exit). Continue on Highway 305S through Poulsbo crossing the Agate Pass Bridge. Turn right on Day Road. Follow the road to the left as it forks onto Miller Road. About 100 yards from the fork is a row of mailboxes and a rockery. After the rockery turn left into Willowbrook's driveway. (206) 842-8034
- Willowbrook Farm is open every weekend in October; Saturdays, 10 am - 5 pm; Sundays, 11 am - 5 pm.
- Admission is FREE; there can be optional expenses.

MAKING MEMORIES

Roast pumpkin seeds together. Rinse seeds from your pumpkin in a colander. Soak overnight in salt water and then dry well. Bake on a cookie sheet at 200° until golden brown. Cool, add butter or salt to taste and they are ready to eat.

HARVEST CARNIVAL

In the Fall, it's time to head to the Harvest Carnival. Try the cake walk, the fishin' hole or the toilet-seat toss. Fill your evening with face painting, making marble art and playing mini-golf. Christ Memorial Church invites you to their annual HARVEST CARNIVAL, October 31. This festive event will have game booths, food and cotton candy for all to enjoy. The games are designed for three different age groups, $1\frac{1}{2}$ to 11 years, so the whole family can have fun!

BEFORE YOU GO
●Help your children think of someone or something they can pretend to be. Create your unique costumes together.

ON THE WAY
●Have the trees changed colors all the way? Did you know when the nights become cooler, the chlorophyll in the leaves begins to break down and that's why the leaves lose their green color? The red, orange and yellow colors were always there; they were just covered up by the green chlorophyll.
●Do you see any spider webs on the trees?

HELPFUL INFORMATION
●The Harvest Carnival is in the Christ the King Academy Gym (across for the Poulsbo library).
●Take Highway 3 to 305S (Poulsbo exit). Continue on Highway 305S and turn west on Lincoln. Christ Memorial Church/Christ the King Academy is on the left. (360) 779-5515
●The carnival is always October 31, 6:30 pm - 8:30 pm.
●Parents need to accompany their children.
●Admission is $1.00; games are 25¢ each.
●Friendly costumes only.

MAKING MEMORIES

For a really fun treat make spider cookies.
What you'll need:
   Oreo cookies
   black licorice
   green gel frosting
Cut the black licorice into eight 1-inch long pieces. Unscrew an Oreo cookie and put the eight legs on the creme. Put the cookie top back on. Use the green gel frosting for eyes and nose.

WATCH THE SALMON RUN

In the fall local creeks come alive as salmon return home. There are several places in Kitsap County to view the incredible SALMON RUN. Watch as huge salmon inch their way up shallow creeks to return to where they were born. In Poulsbo kids can see the salmon on the bridges at Dogfish Creek. In Silverdale salmon can be viewed from Chico Creek and Clear Creek. In Port Orchard, there are good salmon runs at Gorst Creek and at Beaver Creek. Be sure to stay off private property and remind your children not to throw stones or disturb the stream bank. Try to approach the stream slowly and stand still and quiet at the edge. "Fascinating" and "unbelievable" describe this event which your kids will remember for a long while.

BEFORE YOU GO
●Call the Fish & Wildlife Office in late September to get an idea of the different salmons' spawning time. 1-800-215-1979
●Bring polarized sunglasses to help see into the water.
●Leave the dog at home.

ON THE WAY
●Talk about the cycles of nature. Reassure children that the dead salmon are part of the cycle. Did you know nutrients eaten by baby coho come from old salmon carcasses?

HELPFUL INFORMATION
●Creeks that are worth checking out include:
  -Dogfish Creek in Poulsbo; it can be viewed from two bridges inside Valley Nursery on Bond Road off of Highway 305S.
  -Chico Creek in West Bremerton; it can be seen from the bridge on Chico Way or near Golf Club Road.
  -Clear Creek in Silverdale; it can be viewed from the bridge on Bucklin Hill Road.
  -Gorst Creek in Gorst; it is accessible at Otto Jarstad Park off of Sam Christopherson Road.
  -Beaver Creek in Port Orchard; it is just outside the Manchester Fuel Depot on Beach Drive near Beaver Creek Road.

MAKING MEMORIES
Here is a fun salmon story. Start with 10 salmon; they each lay 5,000 eggs in a stream. Half of the eggs are not fertilized. A new road is built nearby and loose soil runs into the stream and kills 1,000 eggs. The rest of the eggs hatch and begin their journey to the ocean. Chemicals from gardens & lawns are carried into the stream and kill 5,000 salmon. 10,000 more are killed by predators like large fish and seagulls. Another 6500 are caught by fishermen. An oil spill kills 1500 more. As they return to spawn, hungry bears catch 450 more. A thoughtless person puts anti-freeze into the stream which kills 500. How many are left to spawn? (50)

JUMP IN THE LEAVES

When was the last time you found yourself buried in a great BIG pile of sweet-smelling autumn leaves? A terrific outdoor adventure of playing in piles of leaves will bring laughter and smiles, making fall memories for your family. With rakes in hand, head to ILLAHEE STATE PARK. Rake, rake, and rake some more!! Soon your pile will be just perfect. Now go for it! Take turns jumping, rolling, hiding, being buried and showering each other with leaves. End your adventure by hiding some candy under the pile and watch those leaves fly!

BEFORE YOU GO
●Wear old comfortable clothes, according to the weather.
●Bring rakes.
●Bring enough candy for everyone. (We suggest keeping the candy a surprise.)

ON THE WAY
●Tell riddles. A riddle is a question that poses a problem for someone to solve. Here are some to try:
    1. What is the little frog's favorite game?
    2. What bird can lift the heaviest weights?
Answers: 1. Hopscotch 2. A crane

HELPFUL INFORMATION
●Illahee State Park is located in Bremerton.
●Take Highway 3 to Highway 303S exit/Waaga Way toward Bremerton. Waaga Way turns into Wheaton Way. Turn left on Sylvan Way. Illahee State Park is on the left near the end of the road.
●Illahee State Park is open year round, dawn to dusk.

MAKING MEMORIES

Help your children create a fall scene.
What you'll need:
    crayon shavings, wax paper
    plain paper (to protect your iron)
    brown construction paper
    iron
Have your children cut out a tree trunk with brown construction paper and place it on a piece of wax paper. They can make crayon shavings, using beautiful fall colors. Sprinkle them around the tree trunk to look like leaves. Cover your picture with another piece of wax paper and a sheet of plain paper. Iron it carefully, using the lowest setting. Hang your children's masterpiece in a sunny window.

WINTER
ADVENTURES

A TREASURED TREE

Make a great memory this holiday season. Pack
up the family and head to a local tree farm for an
adventure in finding your Christmas tree. One
nearby farm is HUBERT'S NOBLE RIDGE TREE
FARM on Seabeck Highway. They have all kinds
of trees, Douglas, Grand, Noble Fir, Pine, Shasta
and a few Norway. Your children can roam the
hills searching for your perfect tree. You'll
be sure to find one you like. Everyone can
warm up afterwards in the Noble House with
complimentary hot apple cider. This wonderful
annual event is a cherished tradition for
many families.

BEFORE YOU GO
- Wear layered clothes and dress warmly. Mittens and a hat are a must.
- Bring a saw or $5 for a saw deposit.
- Bring rope to tie down your tree.

ON THE WAY
- Sing Christmas carols.
- Did you know legend has it that tree decorating began in the 1600's by Martin Luther? He saw trees surrounded by the twinkling stars in the sky. He cut one down, brought it home and decorated it with candles to resemble the stars.

HELPFUL INFORMATION
- Hubert Noble Ridge Tree Farm is located at 4635 Seabeck Highway NW in Seabeck.
- Take Highway 3 to the Newberry Hill exit. Turn west and follow Newberry Hill to the end of the road. Turn left onto Seabeck Highway. Continue on the Highway until you see signs for the tree farm. (360) 373-7044
- The tree farm is open the first Friday after Thanksgiving - December 22, 9 am - 5 pm.
- Trees range from $7.00 and up.

MAKING MEMORIES
Spend an evening watching your favorite Christmas video. While you watch, string a festive garland. Use a large blunt needle to string cranberries, mini marshmallows and bits of orange rind together. After the holidays you can hang this outside for the birds to eat.

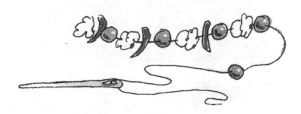

THE PARADE OF BOATS

The waters of Kitsap County light up every December with the Christmas PARADE OF BOATS. Yacht Clubs from Kingston to Port Orchard participate in this delightful tradition. If you don't know someone who lives on the waterfront, you can find a county park or watch from the marinas. You'll see many boats with colorful lights and decorations. Your children can hear personalized greetings from the ships as they pass by. This floating parade of lights will be enjoyed by everyone.

BEFORE YOU GO
●Call ahead, giving your personal greeting to the yacht club in your viewing area. Plan ahead where you will view the parade; this information is needed to personalize your greeting.
●Wear layered clothes and dress warmly. Mittens and a hat are recommended.
●Bring binoculars.

ON THE WAY
●A Parade of Boats is perfect for Kitsap County. Did you know Kitsap Peninsula has 236 miles of saltwater shoreline?

HELPFUL INFORMATION
●The Parade of Boats is usually held the 2nd week of December on Friday and/or Saturday evening.
●Personalized greetings are needed a week in advance.
●For more information call:
  -Bremerton Yacht Club; 2700 Yacht Haven Way, Bremerton, (360) 479-2662
  -Brownsville Yacht Club; 9790 Ogle Road NE, Bremerton, (360) 692-5498
  -Poulsbo Yacht Club; 18129 Fjord Drive Suite T, Poulsbo, (360) 697-9688
  -Port Orchard Yacht Club; P. O. Box 3, Port Orchard, (360) 479-0229
  -Kingston Cove Yacht Club; P. O. Box 81, Kingston, (360) 297-3371

MAKING MEMORIES

On a clear night, spend some time outside looking at the lights in the sky together. Help your children find the big and little dipper. Can you see a shooting star?

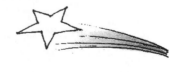

A GIFT TO THE COMMUNITY

Hop in your car and take the family on a drive to Bethlehem. We know a short cut; it won't take long to get there. Silverdale United Methodist Church, along with several other local churches, will help you go back in time with a LIVE NATIVITY ADVENTURE at Christmas. You'll find sheep, donkeys, shepherds and wisemen. Your children can visit with Mary & Joseph, pet the stable animals and listen to the special music. Inside the church you'll find hot chocolate, cider and cookies. Taking this trip to Bethlehem will help you appreciate the gift of Jesus Christ.

BEFORE YOU GO
●Wear layered clothes.
●Find Bethlehem on your world map.
  (It's in the Middle East.)

ON THE WAY
●Talk about traveling in ancient times. (Can you
  imagine riding a long distance on a donkey?)
●Talk about why gifts are given at Christmas.

HELPFUL INFORMATION
●Silverdale United Methodist is located at 9982 Silverdale
  Way in Silverdale.
●Take Highway 3 to the Highway 303S/Silverdale exit,
  staying in your right lane. Travel into Silverdale and
  Silverdale United Methodist is on the corner of Ridgetop
  Boulevard and Silverdale Way.
●The live nativity usually runs the 2nd weekend
  in December. For more information call (360) 692-9813.
●Admission is FREE.

MAKING MEMORIES

Surprise each other this week with a gift of love (a kind word, a helping
hand, an encouraging note or a great big hug).

NEIGHBORHOOD LIGHTS

Watch your children's eyes light up as they see ordinary streets turn into ENCHANTED NEIGHBORHOODS. Take an evening drive and see brilliant displays of holiday cheer. You'll see blue stars, red & white candy canes, and even red Christmas candles as big as a silo. All over Kitsap county, from Port Orchard to Kingston, neighborhoods are waiting for you to view their creativity. After the evening's adventure, end up at home for a cup of hot chocolate.

BEFORE YOU GO
●Wear hats and gloves. (The car windows will be down!)
●Bring Christmas music.
●Bring canned goods. (Some neighborhoods collect
  canned goods for Bremerton Foodline.)

ON THE WAY
●Enjoy Christmas music together.
●Share with each other your favorite houses.
  Why do you like them?

HELPFUL INFORMATION
●Some neighborhoods that are worth checking out include:
  -On Bainbridge Island; Ferncliff NW
  -In North Kitsap; Hostmark Street, Karl Place NE and
   Gamblewood off Bond Road
  -In Central Kitsap; Viewcrest Drive off Sylvan Way,
   Fernwood Court off Trenton Avenue, Twelve Oaks off
   Anderson Hill Road and Steele Creek Mobile Home Park
   off Old Military Road
  -In South Kitsap; Sherlyn Avenue SE off Sedgwick Road,
   Stokes Auction Acres and Regency Drive SE
   off Bethel Road

MAKING MEMORIES

Help your children make beautiful tin can lanterns.
What you'll need:

    a tin can, any size
    hammer and large nail
    masking tape, pencil
    a brown paper bag
Fill each can with water to ¼ inch below the rim and put in the freezer for
about two days, until completely frozen. Use a brown grocery bag and cut
a piece of paper big enough to wrap around the can. Flatten the paper and
have your children draw a simple design with a pencil. Tape the pattern
around the can securely. Place the can on an old, folded towel. Your
children can use a hammer and nail to punch holes in the can along the lines
of the design. Put it back in the freezer if it starts to melt before
they're done. When they're done let the ice melt out and insert a candle.

IT'S SNOW FUN

When the snow comes it's time for a drive to HURRICANE RIDGE for some of the best sledding or inner-tubing around. Pack up the car, and head north for a winter adventure of speed and laughter. Hurricane Ridge has two slide areas for your family. They are the Sunrise Family Snow Play Area and the Tiny Tots Snow Play Area. The hills are just the right size with whoopdies for everyone. The swoosh down is worth the climb back up!

BEFORE YOU GO

- Pack for your family; include extra socks, snacks, thermos, first aid kit, towels, and music for the way.
- Bring your sleds, inner tubes and snow disks. No metal runner sleds, wooden toboggans or snow boards are allowed. No compressed air is available.
- Call for road conditions.

ON THE WAY

- As you travel across the Hood Canal Bridge, see how long your children can hold their breath as you drive across. Did you know that the bridge is over one mile long? No speeding!!
- Talk about snow sledding safety (1 tube at a time, 1 person on a tube, stay with your group, never sled alone, stay in the marked areas, watch out below).

HELPFUL INFORMATION

- Take Highway 3N to Highway 104W across the Hood Canal Bridge. Continue on Highway 104W to Highway 101N. Travel to Port Angeles. Go through Port Angeles and follow signs to Hurricane Ridge (about 17 miles).
- Admission: $10.00 per car, April - November; $10.00 per car only on the weekends, December - March, FREE during the week. (Admission is always good for 7 consecutive days of park use.)
- For more information call (360) 452-0330.

MAKING MEMORIES

Make some snow ice cream. Since snow ice cream is flavored to your taste, vary the proportions until you like it. What you'll need:

    Lots of CLEAN, fresh snow (4 -8 cups)
    cream (1- 2 cups), vanilla (1- 4 tsp.)
    granulated sugar (1-3 cups)

Mix the cream and vanilla together in a small bowl. Layer the snow and granulated sugar in a large chilled bowl. Fold cream mixture into snow, keeping it from draining to the bottom. Toss it gently and eat it as soon as the cream freezes.

SPRING
ADVENTURES

SEE NEW LIFE AT AN OLD FASHIONED FEED STORE

Spring brings new life everywhere: flowers coming up, trees budding and animals being born. Take your family on an adventure to the local FEED STORES to see these baby animals first hand. Newly hatched baby chicks and turkeys are the first adorable animals to arrive in February or March. Next ducklings and baby rabbits can be found when you visit. Your children will delight in seeing these precious animals up close.

BEFORE YOU GO
•Call your local store to ask what animals are in.

ON THE WAY
•Talk about the joy of spring and look for things that are just beginning their life.

HELPFUL INFORMATION
•Some feed stores worth checking out include:
  -Bay Hay & Feed; 10355 NE Valley Road on Bainbridge Island. (206) 842-5274
  -Baxter Farm & Bethel Feed Store; 3855 Bethel Road SE in Port Orchard. (360) 876-4824
  -Bear Creek Country Store; NE 3530 Old Belfair Highway in Belfair. (360) 275-6222
  -Cenex; 20370 Viking Way in Poulsbo. (360) 779-2527
  -Farmland; 9000 Silverdale Way NW in Silverdale. (360) 692-0415
  -Sacks Feed & Garden; 10991 St Highway 104 NE in Kingston. (360) 297-2443

MAKING MEMORIES

Your children can watch new life appear before their very eyes by starting alfalfa seeds. What you'll need:
  alfalfa seeds
  1 jar with a lid with holes punched into it.
Cover the bottom of the jar with seeds. Fill the jar halfway with water. Put the lid on and shake. Empty the water and place the jar on its side. Do this twice a day and in a week the sprouts will come to life. These sprouts are delicious!

DELIGHTFUL
DAFFODILS

Surround yourself with a burst of yellow spring cheer at the ZURN'S TREE AND FLOWER FARM in Belfair. An acre of daffodils are usually blooming during the month of March. As your family walks in the fields, you can pick your own bunch of sunshine. While you're at it, pick an extra bunch to brighten someone else's day. When you're picking, cut only the flower and stem, leaving the green leaves to strengthen the bulb under the ground for next year's flowers.

BEFORE YOU GO
●Bring a pair of scissors for everyone.
●Bring a vases or jar.

ON THE WAY
●Decide with whom you'd like to share your flowers.
●Remind your family that daffodils are poisonous if eaten.

HELPFUL INFORMATION
●Zurn's Tree Farm is located at 9733 West Belfair
Valley Road in Belfair.
●Take Highway 3 to Gorst staying in the right lane. At
Gorst follow signs to Bremerton National Airport(Hwy 3S)
and Belfair. At the first light turn right onto Sam
Christopherson. Go a block and turn left onto the West
Belfair Valley Road. Go 4.2 miles and the farm
is on the left.
●The farm is open only in March, Thursdays, Fridays and
Saturdays, 9 am - 6 pm.
●For more information call (360) 275-2028.
●The gift shop carries crafts and pre-picked flowers.
●Flowers cost $1 for a bunch of ten daffodils.

<table>
<tr><td>

MAKING MEMORIES

When summer bulbs are available, plant some together.
(Gladiolus, onions, and dahlias are some of your choices.)

</td></tr>
</table>

SHEER FUN AT A SHEEP FARM

Bring the children out to the farm and see sheep get sheared. Learn about wool, spinning wheels and other farm animals. While you're there watch the llamas, pet the lambs and enjoy baked goodies. The WOOL HAT FARM'S spring fair is held in April and will be a wooly adventure for all.

BEFORE YOU GO
- Wear comfortable clothes, with sturdy shoes or rubber boots.
- For extra fun, bring your wool hat.

ON THE WAY
- Talk about why sheep are sheared.
- Have your children feel their clothes and describe the different textures.

HELPFUL INFORMATION
- The Wool Hat Farm is located at 2182 NW Rude Road in Poulsbo.
- Take Highway 3 to the Finn Hill exit. Turn west, going over the freeway. Turn left again on Rude Road.
- The Wool Hat Farm's Spring Fair is usually held in April. For more information call (360) 779-4937.
- Tours are available by appointment.
- Admission is FREE; there can be optional expenses.

MAKING MEMORIES

Flock to the kitchen for rice cake lambs to eat. What you'll need:
   rice cakes
   marshmallow creme
   mini marshmallows, chocolate chips, raisins, jelly beans

Cover the top of the rice cake with marshmallow creme. Add wool tuft made from mini marshmallows. Give your lamb two mini chocolate chip eyes, a raisin nose and 2 jellybean ears. Not Baaaad.

FISHING FOR FUN

This adventure will be sure to turn your family into fishing fanatics. The Kitsap Poagie Club sponsors a FISHING DERBY each year on opening day of the fishing season for kids of all ages. Located at Kitsap Lake State Park the club nets a section of the lake in between the piers for kids to try their fishing luck. Kids can fish from the piers or the bank. Everything from poles to bait is provided. The lake is stocked with legal size trout; you may be able to catch dinner. After some fishing fun, have hot chocolate and cookies while you talk about the one that got away.

BEFORE YOU GO

- Wear comfortable clothes, according to the weather.
- Bring a lunch or snacks.
- Bring containers to take your prize fish home in.
- Practice your casting style.

ON THE WAY

- Have your children do finger exercises to get their hands ready for fishing fun.

HELPFUL INFORMATION

- The fishing derby is located at Kitsap Lake Park in Bremerton.
- Take Highway 3 to the Chico Way exit. Go south on Chico Way until it turns to Kitsap Way. Turn right on Harlow Drive and right on Price to Kitsap Lake Park.
- The fishing derby is in April, always held opening day of fishing season, 8 am - 1 pm.
- For more information call (360) 876-9593 or 1-800-215-1979.
- Admission is FREE.

MAKING MEMORIES

Help your children make a fish print. What you'll need:
- a whole fish, cleaned but with the head on
- old newspapers
- tempera paint, large soft brush
- clean sheet of white paper

Lay the fish on a piece of newspaper, and paint the entire fish with the tempera paint. Carefully pick the fish up and place it on another piece of clean newspaper. Lay the clean white paper on the fish, gently rubbing the paper where it covers the fish, being careful not to move the paper. Peel the paper back and lay it, paint side up, flat to dry.

ARMED FORCES DAY PARADE

Picked by residents as the best parade in town, the ARMED FORCES DAY PARADE held in the spring is something your family should not miss. Located in downtown Bremerton, in early May, this festival is said to be the largest Armed Forces Day parade in the nation, honoring men and women of our military. You will see over a hundred entries. Hear talented bands, see elaborate floats, and laugh with the Shrine clowns. Dignitaries will be there, along with crews from submarines and ships. Come early and enjoy the pancake breakfast. Your children can have their faces painted and check out the carnival rides. Have a great day!!

BEFORE YOU GO
●Wear comfortable clothes, according to the weather.
●Bring chairs, blankets or umbrellas if needed.

ON THE WAY
●See how many flags your children can count as you head toward the parade route.
●Talk about the different forces and what each one does. (Army, Navy, Air Force, Marines.)

HELPFUL INFORMATION
●This Festival is held on the Bremerton waterfront.
●Take Highway 3 to Highway 303S exit/Waaga Way toward Bremerton. Waaga Way turns into Wheaton Way which turns into Warren Avenue. After crossing the Warren Avenue Bridge, turn left on 11th Street into the downtown area, parking anywhere.
●Armed Forces Weekend is usually held the 2nd weekend in May.
●The Armed Forces Parade is on Saturday 10 am - noon. The parade starts on Fourth Street and Veneta Avenue and heads toward Warren Avenue. It turns south on Warren, east on Burwell Street, north on Pacific Avenue and west on Sixth Street, ending around Park Avenue.
●For more information call (360) 479-3579.

MAKING MEMORIES
Make a candy card to send or give to a special veteran. What you'll need:
    candy (Extra gum, Lifesavers, U-no, Rocky Road,
    Good & Plenty, Hersheys Hugs and Kisses)
    paper, heavy cardboard (8x10), tape, manila envelope
Start writing the letter on your paper and tape the candy in place of words. Use the cardboard for support. Slide the cardboard and letter into the manila envelope. Hand deliver your candy card. Here is a sample letter: Dear Veteran,
    This letter is to Thank you for the (EXTRA) effort you gave in serving our country. You're a (LIFESAVER).(U-NO) we appreciate the (ROCKY ROAD) you've been down. We hope your day is (GOOD & PLENTY) of love surrounds you. (HUGS & KISSES)

VELKOMMEN TO POULSBO

May 17th marks Norway's Independence Day, which is celebrated in Poulsbo with a VIKING FEST. You don't have to be Norwegian to join in the lutefisk eating contest. See arts & crafts, hear live music and watch Norwegian dancers. Look for the famous Norwegian Fjord Horses on display. Try your skill at kayaking, with a FREE five-minute, "try it you'll like it" paddle on the waterfront. At 2 pm on Saturday enjoy the parade through town. It will be a great day. Velkommen to Poulsbo!

BEFORE YOU GO
●Wear comfortable clothes, according to the weather.
●Bring blankets or umbrellas if needed.

ON THE WAY
●Count how many Norwegian flags you see. Did you know
Norway is ruled by a king and a queen?

HELPFUL INFORMATION
●Take Highway 3 to the Finn Hill exit. Turn right on
Lindvig Way/Front Street and follow it into Old Poulsbo.
●The Viking Fest is usually held the 2nd weekend in May.
For more information call (360) 779 -4848.
●Admission is FREE; there can be optional expenses.
●Olympic Outdoor Center sponsors the kayaking; Saturday
and Sunday; children must be accompanied by an adult.

MAKING MEMORIES

Try some leftse with dinner. It can be found at local grocery stores in the
refrigerator section (it looks like flour tortillas). It is delicious rolled up
with melted butter and a little sugar.

FOREST THEATRE

Hidden next to the 200+ acre Rhododendron Preserve is a unique outdoor theatre which comes alive each Memorial Day weekend during the annual SPRING SHOW OF THE MOUNTAINEER PLAYERS. What started as skits around a campfire has grown into a unique family oriented community outdoor theatre performing fabulous Broadway musicals. The Forest Theatre, built in 1926, is a natural amphitheater just outside Bremerton. The theatre roof is the sky, the walls are the forest, the foundation is the earth and the spotlights are from the sun. The Mountaineers make their Sunday productions very enjoyable for children of all ages.

BEFORE YOU GO
●Bring blankets and cushions to sit on. (Cushions are also available to rent-proceeds to benefit the reserve.)
●Bring snacks or a small picnic.

ON THE WAY
●Sing in the car. What is your favorite musical song?

HELPFUL INFORMATION
●Forest Theatre is located on Seabeck Highway in Seabeck.
●Take Highway 3 to the Chico Way exit. Turn south on Chico Way to Northlake Way. Turn right on Northlake Way; stay to the right when you reach Triangle Imports. At the stop sign turn right onto Seabeck Highway. Parking will be about 1 mile on the right.
●For more information about production titles call The Mountaineer Players (206) 284-6310.
●The Spring show always starts Memorial Day Weekend and has 8 Sunday performances.
●Tickets are available at the Kitsap Mall, Community Theatre in Bremerton or call (206) 284-6310 to charge by phone.
●Admission: (pre-sale) adults - $8.00; children 5-12 - $5.00; (at the trailhead) adults - $9.00; children 5-12 - $6.00; children under 5 are FREE. Check at the ticket booth for family prices.
●Picnic tables and restroom facilities are available in the forest.

MAKING MEMORIES
Turn your day into a musical play. Have fun together as you "sing" all your conversation. For the really creative, write and act out your play at the amphitheater in the Anna Smith Children's Garden in Silverdale. Be sure to invite all your friends and relatives. Award "Oscars" for fabulous performances.

SUMMER ADVENTURES

DESTRUCTION DERBY

During the summer, there's nothing finer than a
night of watching cars race and crash. The
DESTRUCTION DERBY at the Thunderbird
Stadium in Kitsap County is fun for the whole
family. Starting in May your family can pick from
eight different races throughout the summer.
Each race night includes a trophy dash, heat
races, a pit car sponsor race, a special event
figure race and a finale. Kids will delight at the
Big Truck Races, Mini-car football fun, Rollover
Championships, Nostalgia Cars and especially
enjoy the Blindperson race. Time trials start
at 5:30 pm and racing begins at 6:30 pm. Come
early between 4 pm and 5 pm for drivers'
autographs. This adventure will thrill everyone.

BEFORE YOU GO
- Wear layered clothes.
- Bring jackets, blankets or umbrellas if needed.
- Bring comfortable pads or pillows for sitting on.
- Pack a picnic dinner or bring some snacks for the stands. (If you prefer, food is available at the stadium.)
- Bring binoculars.

ON THE WAY
- Be sure to buckle up. Talk about driving safety. Did you know it's a law in Washington state to buckle up?

HELPFUL INFORMATION
- The Destruction Derby is held in the Thunderbird Stadium across from the Fairgrounds in Silverdale.
- Take Highway 3 to Highway 303S exit/Waaga Way. Take Waaga Way to the Central Valley exit and follow signs to the Kitsap Pavillion/Fairgrounds.
- The Destruction Derby runs the 2nd week in May - September, a total of eight races.
- Admission: adults $6.00; military and seniors $5.00; children (6-12) $4.00; children under 6 FREE; family pass (2 adults/3 children) $17.00.
- For more information call (360) 692-3655.

MAKING MEMORIES
Make safety helmets and goggles for your young race drivers.
What you'll need:
    an empty plastic milk gallon jug
    brass fasteners
    construction paper
    tempera paint with comet
    plastic holders from soda can six-packs
    yarn

Cut a helmet shape from the milk jug and attach a strap with construction paper and brass fasteners.
Add a little comet to the tempera paints to help keep the paint on the jug.
Use two plastic circles for goggles. Attach yarn to tie them on. Vrrroom.

ALL ABOARD!

Step back in time to the days of the mighty railroad. Tucked away in the heart of Port Orchard is a great train experience for children, big and small. The KITSAP LIVE STEAMERS TRACK, at South Kitsap Community Park, is a 3,000 ft railroad track which carries a 1/8 scale kid-sized steamer locomotive. Feel the clickety-clack, hear the whistle and see the steam as your children ride around the track and through the woods as many times as they want. Help them imagine traveling to a new land out west. What adventures await them? After the railroad ride, enjoy a frosty mug of old-fashioned rootbeer at Port Orchard's A & W RESTAURANT.

BEFORE YOU GO
●Bring jackets or umbrellas if needed.

ON THE WAY
●Look for train tracks along the way. Encourage your children to imagine where they go.
●Talk about what travel was like before cars.

HELPFUL INFORMATION
●Kitsap Live Steamers is located at South Kitsap Community Park in Port Orchard.
●Take Highway 3 to Highway 16E (Tacoma). Take the Tremont exit turning right off the freeway. Go 2.5 miles (Tremont will turn into Lund) to Jackson. Turn left at Jackson. The entrance to the South Kitsap Community is a block up on the left.
●Admission is FREE; donations are accepted.
●Kitsap Live Steamers runs April - October, the 2nd and 4th Saturday, 10 am - 4 pm (360) 871-6414.
●A & W Restaurant is at 1700 Mile Hill Drive. Turn left out of the park and go .8 miles to Mile Hill Drive. Turn left; A & W is .6 miles on the left. (360) 876-9088

MAKING MEMORIES
Make your own rootbeer. What you'll need:
    3 oz. Rootbeer extract
    4 gallons water
    6 cups sugar
    4-5 lbs. dry ice (Dry ice is
        available at Daily Stop
        in Brownsville
        (360) 692-2073
        with 24 hours' notice.)
Combine all the ingredients
together. Mix for 20 minutes or
until all dry ice is dissolved.
(Be sure not to touch the dry ice
with your bare hands.) Enjoy!

CELEBRATE
SUMMER SOLSTICE

Welcome summer in Scandinavian style. Come for a special day celebrating some Nordic history at the SKANDIA MIDSOMMARFEST held in June. See hundreds of costumed musicians and dancers, view folk craft demonstrations and eat delicious baked goodies. Join everyone in the raising of the "Majstang," a 55-foot pole covered with flowers. Afterwards, enjoy the dancing as fiddlers arm-bend and toetap to polkas, waltzes and other Nordic favorites.

BEFORE YOU GO
●Bring blankets or chairs to sit on.
●Bring sunglasses, hats, jackets or umbrellas if needed.
●Bring water and some snacks.

ON THE WAY
●Did you know in Sweden the festival is celebrated
  on summer solstice, when the country gets nearly
  24 hours of daylight?
●In Sweden the winter is long with little sun,
  so this celebration is especially joyful.

HELPFUL INFORMATION
●Scandia Midsommarfest is held at Raab Park in Poulsbo.
●Take Highway 3 to the Finn Hill exit. Turn right on
  Lindvig Way/Front Street and follow it into Old Poulsbo.
  Travel down Front Street past the stores. Parking is
  available near the waterfront (Anderson Parkway).
  FREE shuttles are provided uphill to Raab Park.
●The midsommarfest is usually held the weekend after
  the first day of summer, 11 am - 6 pm.
●Admission: adults; a $5.00 donation, children under
  12 are FREE.
●For more information call (206) 784-7470.

MAKING MEMORIES

If the sun is shining you can play some fun shadow games with your
children. In shadow tag the
person who is "It" tries to
step on the other player's
shadow. Try touching each
other's shadow hand or
touching a tree's shadow with
your shadow (can your
children touch the very top?).
Try hiding inside someone's
shadow. Have fun in the sun!

BERRY GOOD
BERRY PICKING

Big, red, juicy, delicious. These are words that describe strawberries waiting for you at the OLSON BERRY FARM in Poulsbo. Only two miles from downtown Poulsbo, this family owned farm is one of the few places you can have a strawberry picking adventure. You will be given a row in the two-acre field and you can pick, pick, pick. Your children will delight in discovering and picking luscious strawberries growing abundantly. Bring lots of little helpers so your work is less. The Olson's also sell already picked pints, half flats or full flats of strawberries. Give a gift of strawberries to someone special you know.

BEFORE YOU GO

- Wear comfortable clothes, according to the weather, with sturdy shoes or rubber boots.
- Call for seasonal dates and times.
- No need to bring containers; everything is provided for you.

ON THE WAY

- Talk about all the things you can do with strawberries.
- Talk about picking rules. (Stay in your row, pick as many berries as you can, mark where you stop and treat the plants with care so they will produce again next year.)

HELPFUL INFORMATION

- The Olson Berry Farm is located at 3255 NE Lincoln Road in Poulsbo.
- Take Highway 3 to Highway 305S (Poulsbo exit). Continue on Highway 305S and turn east on Lincoln for 2 miles.
- The strawberry season is usually around the last 3 weeks of June.
- For more information call (360) 779-1737.

MAKING MEMORIES

Make strawberry shortcake for dessert. What you'll need:
- strawberries
- shortcake
- whipped cream

Wash strawberries and mash them up. Cover the shortcake with lots of strawberries and whipped cream. Very simple but very yummy.

FIRE SAFETY DAY

All the fire districts in Kitsap County come together in June for KID'S DAY at the Kitsap County Fairgrounds. This FREE event is great for all children and is a fun time to promote safety in the community. There are puppet shows and clowns to watch and firetrucks and ladders to climb on. See the live demonstrations of the canine unit and be sure to go through the "E.D.I.T.H." house. Kids won't go away empty-handed on this day. They'll take home fire helmets, stamps and stickers, which all include the safety message. This one-day event is sure to exhaust your children but not your pocketbook!

BEFORE YOU GO
●Count the number of smoke detectors in your house.
●Make sure your house number is well marked
 and can easily be seen.
●Find your nearest fire station.

ON THE WAY
●Talk about fire safety. Did you know that "E.D.I.T.H."
 stands for "Exit drills in the house"?

HELPFUL INFORMATION
●Fire Safety Day is held at the Fairgrounds in Silverdale.
●Take Highway 3 to Highway 303S exit/Waaga Way. Take
 Waaga Way to Central Valley Road exit and follow the
 signs to the Kitsap Pavillion/Fairgrounds. Fire Safety Day
 is held in the Presidents Hall.
●Fire Safety Day is usually held the
 2nd or 3rd week in June.
●Admission is FREE.
●For more information call (360) 692-0880.

MAKING MEMORIES

Make an escape plan for your home. Practice it on the first day of
each month (the same day you check your smoke detectors).

MEET
HERE

FOLLOW THE FOOT FERRY TO THE FARMER'S MARKET

Take those feet of yours down to the FARMER'S MARKET in Port Orchard. Blow bubbles as you travel across the Sinclair Inlet on the foot ferry. Docking in Port Orchard, you'll find unique, handcrafted arts and crafts, farm fresh food and music. Look at all the fresh flowers and colorful produce. Take a "color" walk and see if your children can find every color in nature. Yellow, violet, blue, white, red, pink, green, brown and black are just some of the colors you'll see.

BEFORE YOU GO
●Wear layered clothes and bring a jacket.
●Bring a bottle of blowing bubbles for the ferry ride.

ON THE WAY
●The foot ferry ride can be lots of fun, blowing bubbles and counting how many Navy ships are in Sinclair Inlet.
●Did you know that the Port Orchard Farmer's Market is one of the largest farmer's markets in the state?

HELPFUL INFORMATION
●The foot ferry departs from the Bremerton waterfront and arrives to the farmers market located on the Port Orchard waterfront
Take Highway 3 to Highway 303S exit/Waaga Way towards Bremerton. Waaga Way turns into Wheaton Way, which turns into Warren Avenue. After crossing Warren Avenue Bridge, turn left on 11th Street and follow signs to ferry. You can find FREE parking along the street or pay lots are available.
●Boats leave every 30 minutes from 6:30 am to 12:30 am (360) 876-2300.
●This 10-minute ride is FREE on Saturdays and Sundays, May - October.
●The Farmer's Market is open April - September, Saturdays, 9 am - 3 pm, (360) 876-3073.

MAKING MEMORIES
Make vegetable prints with vegetables you found at the farmer's market.
What you'll need:
   apples, green bell peppers,
   mushrooms, cabbage, lemons
   and a bunch of celery
   tempera paints
   clean white paper

Pour diluted tempera paint on a plate. Cut vegetables in half and dip in paint. Place prints on white paper for a lovely design. A celery bunch crosscut 2 inches from the end makes a beautiful rose design.

BOOMERFEST

The Naval Submarine Base at Bangor opens its gates to the public during the annual BOOMERFEST held in the summer. Kids will enjoy a parade, facepainting, game booths, carnival rides, go carts and the FREE Wenatchee Youth Circus. There's also live music, arts & crafts, submarine memorabilia and ethnic food. For bike riders of all ages there is a FREE mountain bike challenge at Trident Lakes with divisions for all levels of experience. Ride a 1-mile flat track or try the progressive hill climb. This all-day event is packed with things the whole family can get excited about, thanks to our military neighbors.

BEFORE YOU GO
●Wear comfortable clothes, according to the weather.
●Bring a lunch or snacks.
●Plan your transportation to Boomerfest. Shuttles
  are available from the mall and there are
  easy parking places on base.

ON THE WAY
●Talk about what the name "Boomerfest" could mean.
●Did you know a '"Boomer" is the only type of submarine
  that has the ability to carry strategic missiles?

HELPFUL INFORMATION
●Boomerfest is held on the Bangor Naval Submarine Base.
●Take Highway 3 to the Naval Submarine Base
  Bangor/Ordnance exit. The base is open to the public this
  day only. Maps are available on the base.
●Boomerfest is usually held in the last week
  in June, 10 am - 10 pm.
●Admission is FREE; there can be optional expenses.
●For more information call (360) 779-5866.

MAKING MEMORIES

Make a submarine or 'boomer' sandwich together!

FIREWORKS ON THE FJORD

Join your neighbors in celebrating our nation's birthday. Come to Poulsbo's waterfront on July 3rd for a spectacular fireworks display over Liberty Bay. Hear the Navy band play patriotic music as you watch the 40-minute show. There will be lots of oohs and aahs at the FIREWORKS ON THE FJORD. Bring some "pop" corn for an extra fun snack.

BEFORE YOU GO
●Wear layered clothes and bring a jacket.
●Bring chairs and blankets, or umbrellas if needed.
●Come early for good seats.

ON THE WAY
●Count how many flags you see as you drive to Poulsbo.
●What do the colors and shapes represent?

HELPFUL INFORMATION
●Fireworks can be viewed from Poulsbo's
  waterfront park.
●Take Highway 3 to the Finn Hill exit. Turn right on
  Lindvig Way/Front Street and follow it into Old Poulsbo.
  Travel down Front Street past the stores.
●Parking is near the waterfront park (Anderson Parkway).
●Fireworks usually start at 10:30 pm.

MAKING MEMORIES

Make a fireworks picture. What you'll need:
    paper
    watercolor paint
    straws
Put a few drops of paint onto the paper. Use a straw to blow the paint,
creating a firework pattern on the paper.

THE TINY TOWN OF KINGSTON

Come see a TINY TOWN CELEBRATION in the
not so tiny town of Kingston. The weekend of the
4th of July is filled with a parade, daily events
on the main stage and a complete miniature town
for kids to go in. This tiny town is found in the
Kola Kole Park and has remarkable detail. Your
children can shop in the Thriftway store and make
an imaginary pizza at the Pizza Factory. The
family stage features music, dancers and puppet
presentations. There are craft and food booths,
inflatable rides and an ice cream eating contest.
For little ones, don't miss the Little Folks Park
and the train ride. To end the celebration enjoy
the classic car show at the Marina Park.

BEFORE YOU GO
●Wear comfortable clothes, according to the weather.
●Bring blankets or umbrellas if needed.

ON THE WAY
●A tiny town is like a small community. Talk about the benefits of living in a small community. What are some responsibilities?

HELPFUL INFORMATION
●Tiny Town is located in Kola Kole Park in Kingston.
●Take Highway 3 to 305S (Poulsbo exit). Continue on Highway 305S and go left at Bond Road (307N). Bond Road continues into Kingston. Parking is wherever you can find it.
●The parade is always held on the 4th, in between ferry runs. For more information call (360) 297-3813.

MAKING MEMORIES

Help your children make a tiny town. What you'll need:
   a drainage saucer for a 10" flower pot
   fresh potting soil
   wheat berries or rye grass seed
   clear plastic wrap
   spray bottle of water
   miniature toys: Lego men, blocks, twigs, cars

Fill the saucer with potting soil. Sprinkle the wheat berries or rye grass on the whole area. Spray lightly with the water until it is damp and cover with the plastic wrap. Keep it out of direct sun and moist until the seeds germinate (4-5 days) After the seeds have germinated take the plastic wrap off and put your town near a sunny window. The seeds will sprout fast! Your children can make pathways or streets by clipping the grass, add homes, cars, twigs and flowers. Now your children have their own tiny town!

FOR A WHALE
OF A DAY

Silverdale comes alive the last weekend of July. Old Town overflows with the sights of art and crafts, smells of exotic food and sounds of live entertainment. WHALING DAYS is a community event not to be missed. Come on Saturday for a delightful parade, which starts at 10 am. Sunday afternoon your children can cheer for your own sponsored rubber duck in "The Great Kitsap Duck Race." In the evening you'll all enjoy watching the firework displays over the Silverdale Bay.

BEFORE YOU GO
- Sponsor a rubber duck in the race. This event benefits over 30 different programs for the Silverdale community.
- Wear comfortable clothes, according to the weather.
- Bring chairs and blankets, or umbrellas if needed.

ON THE WAY
- Did you know the early founders of Silverdale wanted to call this town Goldendale, but found the name already taken? So instead of using the word "gold" they used the word "silver" and called their town "Silverdale."

HELPFUL INFORMATION
- Whaling Days is held in Silverdale.
- Take Highway 3 to Highway 303S/Silverdale exit. Go south on Kitsap Mall Boulevard. Take the first right and you can park in the Kitsap Mall parking lot.
- Whaling Days is always the last full weekend in July.
- The parade starts at Target, comes down Kitsap Mall Boulevard, turns right onto Silverdale Way, and ends at Anderson Hill Road.
- Food, crafts and entertainment are at Silverdale Waterfront Park.
- The Great Kitsap Duck Race is on Sunday at 3 pm. For more information call (360) 698-0576.

MAKING MEMORIES

To encourage creative thinking and spontaneity, have a pajama run. After the kids are all tucked in bed, (but before they nod off to sleep), surprise them by yelling "Pajama Run" as you run through the house. Gather your startled family into the car and head to your favorite ice cream drive-through restaurant. Order a small treat and enjoy your silly evening outing together.

CROSBY DAZE

Join this rural town south of Silverdale in celebrating their annual Heritage Festival, CROSBY DAZE, in August. This event is very casual; the parade starts at 10 am (if you show up 'round 9 you can probably be in it if you want!). There's a pole toss and chainsaw competitions, kids' games, a quilt auction, pie-baking contests and chicken Bingo. Look at handmade crafts and a vintage car show. Stay for the Sawdust Dance at the Crosby Community Center, the oldest community center in Washington. Stop in at the CAMP UNION COOKHOUSE for homemade pie or soup. Enjoy country atmosphere and see many historical items all over the walls and ceiling. Do you see the rocking chair in the rafters? Can your children find the petrified dinosaur dung?

BEFORE YOU GO
●Wear your country jeans, suspenders, and flannel shirt,
with comfortable walking shoes.

ON THE WAY
●Enjoy the rural drive up and down hills and notice
the different kinds of trees growing.
●Did you know Crosby is a living-history community?
There are five generations of families living in
this delightful town.

HELPFUL INFORMATION
●Crosby Daze is held in Crosby.
●Take Highway 3 to the Newberry Hill exit. Turn west
and follow Newberry Hill to the end of the road.
Turn left on Seabeck Highway. Take a right on Holly
Road. Travel to Camp Union Cookhouse at
14194 NW Holly Road. (360) 830-5298
●Crosby Daze is usually the first week in August.
●Admission is FREE; there can be optional expenses.
●For more information call (360) 830-5737.
●The parade starts at the Camp Union Cookhouse,
goes up the road, then left for 1.9 miles to
Crosby Community Center on Christopher Road.

MAKING MEMORIES

Design three different quilt patterns;
one using triangles,
one using squares and
one using circles.

WHO WAS CHIEF SEATTLE?

This adventure is rich in native history. CHIEF SEATTLE DAYS is an annual festival in Suquamish, celebrating the Suquamish Indians in Kitsap County. The August weekend brings the special remembrance of tradition in the dramatic drum and dance festivities, an authentic salmon bake and canoe races. Children will enjoy searching for CHIEF SEALTH'S (Seattle's) grave in a small cemetery behind St. Peter's Catholic Church. Afterwards drive towards the Agate Pass Bridge and stop to learn more about totem poles and their stories.

BEFORE YOU GO
- Can you find the Port Madison Indian Reservation in your telephone book map? Did you know the Suquamish people once occupied much of Kitsap Peninsula?

ON THE WAY
- Look for Northwest Indian symbols.
- Did you know totem poles tell a story?

HELPFUL INFORMATION
- Chief Seattle Days is held in Suquamish.
- Take Highway 3 to Highway 305S (Poulsbo exit). Continue on Highway 305S through Poulsbo. Past Poulsbo, turn left on Suquamish Way to go into Suquamish.
- Chief Seattle's grave is behind St. Peter's Catholic Church (watch for signs).
- Chief Seattle Days is usually held the last weekend in August.
- Admission is FREE; there can be optional expenses.
- For more information call (360) 598-3311.

MAKING MEMORIES

Make a fun celery totem pole snack. What you'll need:
    celery
    cream cheese or peanut butter
    gummy bears, gummy fish
Cut 4-inch celery pieces. Fill with cream cheese or peanut butter. Place your gummy bears and gummy fish on the celery. Stand the celery up for a totem pole snack. Make up a story about your totem pole.

REALLY BIG TRUCKS!

Big kids and little kids both will enjoy this opportunity to see close up all kinds of BIG vehicles. You'll see firetrucks, army trucks, street cleaners and busses. Go inside ambulances, tow trucks and sit on a motorcycle. Steer 16-wheelers and control a huge cement mixer arm. All kinds of fun is waiting for you during Poulsbo's TOUCH A TRUCK in August. This hands-on (or bodies-on) event is sure to be a great memory for this summer. Afterwards, walk across the street to MITZEL'S for delicious pie.

BEFORE YOU GO

- Wear comfortable clothes, according to the weather.
- Bring your camera for fun pictures of your children imagining their future job.

ON THE WAY

- Count how many trucks you see on the way.
- Look at all the different kinds and sizes of wheels.

HELPFUL INFORMATION

- Touch a Truck is held at Poulsbo Village Shopping Center in Poulsbo.
- Take Highway 3 to Highway 305S (Poulsbo exit). Continue on Highway 305S through 3 lights to Poulsbo Village Shopping Center on the right.
- Touch a Truck is usually held the 2nd week of August, 11 am -3 pm.
- Admission is FREE.
- For more information call (360) 779-4848.
- Mitzel's is next door, 760 NE Liberty Road.

MAKING MEMORIES

Your children can make a collage of trucks using magazine pictures.

COUNTY FAIR FUN

Did you know that your children can enter things in the KITSAP COUNTY FAIR? Their collections (Legos, dolls, keys), art work, photographs and more are all welcome for display, during the county fair which is usually the last week in August. By entering your special objects and paying an exhibitor's fee, you can receive a complimentary five-day exhibitor's pass to enjoy the fair all week. Plan ahead for a good time.

BEFORE YOU GO

- Pick up a Premium Book (with rules of entry).
- Enter your special exhibits the Saturday and Sunday before the fair. Entries of fresh produce and/or flowers are taken on Monday before the fair.
  Check the premium book for special hours.
- To help you get into the spirit of the fair, read the book or watch the video "Charlotte's Web."
- Wear comfortable clothes and bring a jacket.

ON THE WAY

- Talk about what things you want to see at the fair.
  Look for Zuckerman's famous pig.

HELPFUL INFORMATION

- Premium Books are available in mid-June at the libraries, feed stores, Chambers of Commerce and the Fairground's office at 1200 NW Fairgrounds Road. (360) 692-3655
- Kitsap County Fair is held at the Fairgrounds in Silverdale.
- Take Highway 3 to Highway 303S exit/Waaga Way.
  Take Waaga Way to Central Valley Road exit and follow the signs to Kitsap Pavillion/Fairgrounds.
- The fair is usually held the third week in August.
- The exhibitor's fee is: adults - $5.00; children - $2.00.
  (This fee entitles the exhibitor to a five-day pass.)
- Kids' day is usually Wednesday.

MAKING MEMORIES

Help your children start a collection for next year's fair. How about heart rocks or gum wrappers? Maybe your children can be creative and collect something unusual like hats, footprints or autographs! Think of fun ways to display the collection.

Every effort has been made to ensure the accuracy of the information contained in this book. If we blundered, please write and let us know. Do you have a fun family adventure? We are collecting material for the next edition and invite your comments and ideas.

R & R Publications
P. O. Box 133
Silverdale, WA 98383-0133

ORDER FORM

Qty	Title	Price	Total
	Great Adventures for Kitsap Peninsula	$9.95	
	Subtotal		
	Sales Tax 8.1% (Add 81¢ for each book)		
	Postage & Handling (Add $1.75 for one book, 50¢ for each additional book)		
	Total Enclosed		

Your name _____

Address _____

City _____

State _____ Zip _____

Daytime Phone _____

Make checks payable to: R & R Publications
Send to: Great Adventures for Kitsap Peninsula
P. O. Box 133
Silverdale, WA 98383-0133

Thanks for your order.
Have some great adventures together!!